HOW TO DISCIPLE MEN

(SHORT AND SWEET)

45

PROVEN STRATEGIES

FROM EXPERTS ON

MINISTRY TO MEN

FROM THE NATIONAL COALITION OF MINISTRIES TO MEN

Foreword by
PATRICK MORLEY

Jay Payleitner and David Murrow, EDITORS

BroadStreet
PUBLISHING

BroadStreet Publishing® Group, LLC
Racine, Wisconsin, USA
BroadStreetPublishing.com

HOW TO DISCIPLE MEN (SHORT AND SWEET):
45 PROVEN STRATEGIES FROM EXPERTS ON MINISTRY TO MEN

CONTENTS

HOW DO YOU DISCIPLE A MAN?

H ow do you disciple a man? *Introduce him to Jesus. Get him into a small group. Teach him to pray and read his Bible daily. Help him deal with his issues. Get him serving others.* But what else?

Everybody knows *what* men's ministry is supposed to accomplish; most Christians understand *why* men need Jesus. The problem is the *how.* How do we build and sustain ministry to men? How do we get men to take the next step toward wholeness? How do we deal with the frustrations and challenges that always seem to crop up?

When we began assembling chapters for this book, we asked our authors to focus on the *hows* of men's ministry. We asked for short chapters that were packed with practical advice that would help men draw other men to Christ. We asked for solutions, not sermons.

The forty-five authors who contributed to this book possess well over a thousand years of combined ministry experience. They're the world's foremost experts on ministry to men. So benefit from their advice. Learn from their mistakes. Profit from their wisdom.

We chose to keep the chapters "short and sweet" so you could quickly find the advice you need in any given situation. You may choose to read the book as a whole, or simply take a chapter a day for a month and a half of inspiration. It's up to you.

If you find this book helpful, here are three things you can do:

1. *Join the National Coalition of Ministries to Men (NCMM).* If you disciple men, NCMM is your tribe. Come alongside hundreds of courageous disciple makers who share your vision for men. Learn more at ncmm.org.

vi | HOW TO DISCIPLE MEN

2. *Contact our authors.* If you benefitted from a particular chapter, the contributor would love to hear from you. Don't be shy. Send a note of thanks, begin a dialogue, or avail yourself of any resources, such websites. Use the contact information at the beginning of each chapter to get in touch with the authors.

3. *Pray for and promote this book.* Would the senior pastor or men's pastor at your church benefit from reading this book? Do you know a friend or colleague who ministers to men, either full-time, part-time, or as a faithful volunteer? Give it as a gift. And please pray that God uses this book to advance his kingdom work among men around the world.

—Jay Payleitner and David Murrow

FOREWORD

(PATRICK MORLEY)

Patrick Morley is the founder and executive chairman of Man in the Mirror, a ministry focused on helping every church disciple every man. He is the author of more than twenty books, including *The Man in the Mirror*. For more information, visit maninthemirror.org.

My favorite thing to do is getting to know men one-on-one over coffee or a meal. Over the last four decades, I've met with thousands of men in this way. It has been my greatest honor and highest privilege in ministry.

A lot of men I meet in that context are hurting. When I ask them to put into words what they feel is holding them back—from feeling fully alive—they inevitably mention one or more of seven inner aches and pains:

- I just feel like I'm in this alone.
- I don't feel like God cares about me personally—not really.
- I don't feel like my life has a purpose—it feels random.
- I have these destructive behaviors that keep dragging me down.
- My soul feels dry.
- My most important relationships are not healthy.
- I don't feel like I'm doing anything that will make a difference and leave the world a better place.

Here's the thing: Every day, these men are driving to and from work on streets that pass by your church. And every now and then, one of them will look over and think, *I wonder if that's a place where I could find some answers?*

Meanwhile, inside the church, the staff and different groups of leaders often meet to think and strategize about how to get more men into church, and how to more effectively disciple the ones they already have. But they're frustrated they can't seem to sustain any long-term momentum. That's why this book exists—to help you help them.

The book you are holding is a remarkable achievement. Consider this: Forty-five of the world's most talented and experienced men's discipleship experts were asked, "If you could only say one thing to a leader who wants to disciple men more effectively, what would it be?" The consolidated wisdom of these forty-five experts represents a tour de force on the subject of men's discipleship.

Men's discipleship is especially important to me. As I wrote in *Pastoring Men,* I am so grateful that when my wife and I first visited church as newlyweds, several mature Christian men were on the look-out for younger guys like me. Knowing what needed to be done, they took me under their wings and began to disciple me into biblical man-hood and, from the start, gave me the vision to disciple other men—to become not only a disciple, but a "disciple-making disciple."

Hugh Lake preached the gospel with simplicity and clarity. H. O. Giles and Bob Helmling walked out their faith in such an authentic way that my resistance melted away. Then God used Dan Stanley to bring me to conviction of sin during a young couples' class one Sunday morning by simply reading from God's Word (Ephesians 5:25, to be specific). Next, Jim Gillean invited us to be part of his small group, where my wife, Patsy, and I were equipped.

Jim saw something in me I didn't see in myself. What really struck me was how he believed in me more than I believed in myself. He spoke words of encouragement I'd never heard. That unchained some-thing inside me. He showed me how I could become the man God created me to be. His faith in me released the power to become a man I didn't even know was "in there." He started me down a path to become the man I wanted to be—a godly man, husband, father, and disciple maker.

God has given us a clear, simple prescription to bring men to maturity. That is for mature men, like Jim, to take younger men, like me, under their wings and show them how to walk the Christian life. Why? *Because it takes a man to teach a man how to be a man.*

By all means, let's continue helping single moms, pregnant teenagers, and fatherless boys. We need more of that, not less. But we'll never solve these symptomatic problems without treating the underlying cause—that men don't understand biblical manhood. Making disciples is God's designated way to release the power of his gospel on every problem men face.

In a real sense, the cure for everything starts with men's discipleship. The bottom line is this: However we got ourselves into our current situation, the only solution is to disciple our way out. But men are not going to become disciples just because we think it's "really, really important." Like anything worthwhile, it takes knowledge, expertise, skill, and experience. The Holy Spirit usually does his best work when people know what they're doing.

When God puts a man who is stuck in your path, discipleship means finding out why and then helping him solve his problem. This book will equip you with forty-five tangible ways to effectively help that man solve his problem.

Here's the good news: If we get men right, we will get marriages right too. If we get marriages right, then we will get families right. If we get families right, we will get church right. And if we get church right, then God will change the world. This is a battle that, together, we can win. We cannot, we must not, and, by God's grace, we will not fail.

Section I

THE CASE FOR MINISTRY TO MEN

1

THE KEYS TO DISCIPLING EVERY MAN IN YOUR CHURCH

(BRETT CLEMMER)

Brett Clemmer is the president of Man in the Mirror, a ministry focused on helping every church disciple every man. Man in the Mirror was founded by Patrick Morley, the author of *The Man in the Mirror*. Brett lives in Casselberry, Florida, with his wife; they have two young-adult children. Learn more at maninthemirror.org.

Quickly answer these two questions: (1) How many men are in your church? (2) How many men are in the men's ministry?

A conventional mind-set defines "men's ministry" as only those guys who show up for the weekly men's groups, monthly breakfast, and annual men's retreat. Break out of that thinking and consider a new idea: an all-inclusive ministry to men.

This all-inclusive ministry to men approach is based on two overriding principles: First, God has called us to disciple every willing man in the church and community, not just those who are currently coming to men's-only events. Second, everything that any man does with your church is ministry to men. An all-inclusive ministry to men maximizes the kingdom impact of every interaction with every man, no matter the setting.

Make a list of all the places men participate in your church, such as: worship service, nursery, ushers, Sunday School teachers, deacons, elders, parking lot ministry, softball team, and sound booth. Now think of it this way: Every one of those men is part of your ministry to men!

Instead of focusing on how many men you can get to your men's-only events, strategize ways to help every ministry that touches men to disciple those men right where they are. Help the head usher get his men talking about Scripture and praying for each other. Tell the men working in the nursery how much you appreciate their ministry to the babies and parents they serve. Get some mature Christian guys to join the softball team and develop relationships with guys behind them on their spiritual journey.

Our goal as men's leaders is not to build a program, but to build disciples. Why not think of every opportunity the church has to help men grow and serve, rather than just the men's-only activities?

THREE PROBLEMS SOLVED

Have you heard of the 80/20 rule? It says that 20 percent of the people participate in 80 percent of the ministry. This often leads to ministry leaders "chasing" the same people to try to get them involved.

However, having an all-inclusive ministry to men mind-set helps eliminate "turf wars" with other ministries within your church. You are no longer pursuing the same group of already-busy men. Instead, your leadership team is looking around for ministries that are reaching men successfully and then helping any way they can.

One church men's team was frustrated because all the young fathers in their church were participating in the family ministry activities and never coming to men's events. They were helping in AWANA, coaching in the sports leagues, going to the marriage class, and eventually serving in leadership positions, all without ever being involved in the "men's ministry." With a little coaching, they realized there was a whole group of men they could reach through the family ministry. So they got behind it to see how they could help the family ministry be even more effective at reaching men.

This points to a solution for another problem: an all-inclusive mind-set takes the pressure off your team members to reach every man all by themselves. Look around the church for ministries that are serving men well, and then identify the gaps—groups of men who aren't being reached. You can focus your planning efforts there, while supporting the other ministries that are already reaching men.

I was sitting around a campfire at a men's retreat several years ago. I turned to the head usher from my church and said, "You know, you lead the largest ministry for men in the church." He quickly explained that he wasn't part of the men's ministry; rather, he was the head usher. Quickly, I pointed out to him that more men participated on the usher teams than any other ministry in the church. And then I challenged him, "What are you doing to disciple them?"

He had never thought of that before. In response to my challenge, we developed a strategy to help the guys begin to memorize a verse together, pray for each other, and check in with one other usher on the team every week. Fifty men suddenly had a leader who was excited about helping them grow in their faith, and the men's leadership team could focus its efforts on *other* guys.

Finally, an all-inclusive mind-set puts you on the pastor's team. Many books have been written about overcoming "ministry silos." Too often, ministry leaders (not just men's ministry) want to build a "mini-church" within the church for the group they are focused on. With this approach, the men's leadership team can contact the pastor and say, "We want to get on board with what's working already, not create a bunch of new activities." Your pastor will love it!

HOW TO GET STARTED

Changing your mind-set from "men's ministry" to "helping men become discipled wherever they are involved" can be difficult. It's important to get your men's leaders on board with the idea. I suggest you share this chapter with them and then start to brainstorm. Ask, "Where are the men in our church already involved?" Make a list of all the ministries you can think of, and what type of men are involved: their ages, spiritual maturity, and family situation. This will help you identify opportunities as well as gaps—certain types of men who are not engaged in growth or service opportunities.

Next, brainstorm ways you could reach the men in these ministries. Think outside the box. One church realized that many unchurched men came to family night during vacation Bible school, so they organized games in the lobby before and during the break, and stationed leaders to run the games and meet the dads to invite them to a men's BBQ. Help the Upward Sports or AWANA programs recruit men to coach, referee, and listen to Bible verses. Recruit men to work with teenage boys in the youth group.

Finally, plan to approach the leaders of the ministries that are recruiting and deploying men at your church. Meet them at church or take them out for coffee. Then offer to help: "I'm on the men's leadership team, and we've noticed that your ministry is doing a great job of reaching men. We're excited about men being discipled, no matter where they are involved in the church. How can we help you and your ministry?"

A RADICAL IDEA

Every man in your church is part of your ministry to men. In fact, just abandon the phrase "men's ministry" altogether. It usually conjures up a picture of a bunch of guys eating pancakes anyway, rather than bold, faithful disciples passionately pursuing Christ.

Instead, develop a disciple-making ministry to every man in your church. Help leaders who are already engaged with men be more effective. Focus on identifying gaps—unreached men in the church—and target new ministry efforts toward them. Focus on how you can maximize the kingdom potential of every interaction your church has with every man.

For more information, go to maninthemirror.org and search for "all-inclusive." Or check out the book *No Man Left Behind*, where you'll find a chapter on this topic, as well as more strategic insights on building a sustainable ministry to every man in your church.

2

WHY MEN MUST DISCIPLE THEIR FAMILIES

(BRIAN DOYLE)

Brian Doyle serves as founder, CEO, and president of Iron Sharpens Iron, which equips churches to train men for spiritual leadership. He oversees the ISI Network, which hosts equipping conferences for men around the nation. Brian also serves on the board of directors for the National Coalition of Ministries to Men and The Fatherhood CoMission. Contact Brian at ironsharpensiron.net.

We live in a professional culture where trained experts mow our lawns, change the oil in our cars, care for our young children, cook our food, and paint our houses. Many men in this professional culture have learned to hire others to do what their fathers and grandfathers did themselves.

Under this twenty-first-century model, the American father fulfills the role of general contractor for his family. Merriam-Webster. com defines a general contractor as "a person or business entity that contracts to be in charge of a building project usually involving the use of subcontractors." The modern man hires professionals to teach his children, coach their athletics, and tutor them in academics. And he "hires" the local church to take care of his family's spiritual needs.

The modern man tends to see church staff and trained volunteers as most qualified to help his family come to a saving faith in Christ and grow as disciples. The church staff takes care of his family's spiritual development, which means there is no need for him to do this work. Men gladly hand this responsibility off to church professionals, breathing a prayer of thanks to God for their local church. This may sound like a win-win scenario, but in fact it is almost always lose-lose.

God's design is that the family should be the primary place of discipleship, and that men lead that effort. Moses shared these words with the men in Deuteronomy 6:4–7:

> Hear, O Israel: The LORD our God, the LORD is one. Love the LORD your God with all your heart and with all your soul and with all your strength. These commandments that I give you today are to be on your hearts. Impress them on your children. Talk about them when you sit at home and when you walk along the road, when you lie down and when you get up.

Teaching God's Word must happen in and around the home. It is best shared in the rhythm of daily life.

Pastors and church leaders often lament the fact that most the men in the church are disengaged. They complain that the men are not hungry for God and not passionate to grow as Christ followers. They are discouraged that their men do not stand tall as ambassadors for Christ in the marketplace.

The truth is that many Christian men who are part of a local church are disengaged because the local church has disengaged them. This is because the church is fulfilling the role meant for the man. Church leaders are called to not only do ministry, but to equip others to do ministry. Paul shares in Ephesians 4:11–12, "And he gave the apostles, the prophets, the evangelists, the shepherds and teachers, to equip the saints for the work of ministry, for building up the body of Christ" (ESV). This admonition stands in contrast to the professional contractor model of the twenty-first century. In this model, the church staff and leadership are the "ministers," and the congregation is there to support them in the work.

Church leaders do have a special responsibility in addition to equipping the saints for works of service, and that is to "shepherd the flock." Peter gives this instruction to church leaders in 1 Peter 5:1–3:

> To the elders among you, I appeal as a fellow elder and a witness of Christ's sufferings who also will share in the glory to be revealed: Be shepherds of God's flock that is under your care, watching over them—not because you must, but because you are willing, as God wants you to be; not pursuing dishonest gain, but eager to serve; not lording it over those entrusted to you, but being examples to the flock.

Who makes up the flock that is under your care? Is everyone who attends church services on the weekend under your direct care? Is it limited to those who have completed a membership class and joined as members? Does it include men and women, old and young, new in the faith, and established in the faith?

You may wonder why I am asking these questions in a book about men's ministry. Could it be that the reason men are so disengaged is because of the way we view those we are called to shepherd? How do you see the men who attend your church? Are they part of your general constituency or do they have a unique role? Is your responsibility to the men of your local church different or the same as it is to the women, youth, and children who attend your church?

If a family of six begins to attend your church services on a regular basis, are all six part of the flock that God has called you to shepherd? If yes, would this be direct or indirect shepherding? This family includes a man, a woman, and four minor children, and all of them need to know Christ and grow as his disciples. Your church likely has something specific to offer each family member, but the question remains: Are they all equally under your care?

Before you answer this question, consider the signals we as church leaders may be sending to members of our congregations. Let's consider four different measures and what they each may communicate to God's flock that is under our care:

1. *Church staff:* What areas of church ministry are covered by church staff? We invest significant resources and hire

trained professionals for certain areas of specific ministry, but not for other areas of ministry. What does this communicate?

2. *Church programs:* What people groups in our church have the most-developed programs available to them? What programs are the most visible in our local church? What does this communicate?

3. *Church calendar:* What are the events and meetings on your church calendar this week and next week and into the future? What events for what demographics tend to dominate your church calendar year after year? What does this communicate?

4. *Church budget:* Where do we invest our finances? We teach what Jesus said, "For where your treasure is, there your heart will be also" (Matthew 6:21). Where are we investing our treasure? Where is our heart? What does this communicate?

Let's go back to that family of six who begins to attend your church on a regular basis. If there is a man in that group, he is likely the husband and father. Almighty God has given him responsibility for the spiritual growth of his wife and children. It's likely he does not even know this. Your church can graciously and intentionally begin to build this man with others in mind. Your investment into this man will quickly benefit his wife, their marriage, and their four children.

Your church-based men's ministry is far more significant than helping men who seem resistant to help. By ministering to men, you are choosing to operate according to God's design, being intentional about God's order. You are building men with others in mind. You certainly can and should have exceptional children's ministry and youth ministry at your church. But I implore you to also have an exceptional church-based ministry to men. This is the only place a man will get the training he needs to be a spiritual leader. This spiritual leadership will most often start in the home, but then move outside of the home as he becomes an ambassador for Christ in the marketplace. He must first, though, be an ambassador for Christ in his own home.

The rest of this book takes away the mystery of what this looks like and is filled with tips and nuggets that will help your church become a training center for godly men. May almighty God show you much favor as you align with his purposes and intentions.

3

AN IMPORTANT MESSAGE FOR THE SENIOR PASTOR

(VINCE D'ACCHIOLI)

Vince D'Acchioli is the founder and CEO of On Target Ministries (OTM). Vince's seminar for senior pastors deals with "The Six Structural Elements of Effective Churches" and has been shared in numerous places throughout North America. For more information regarding OTM and their resources, please visit otm.co.

Over the past twenty-five years, I've put on men's events in hundreds of churches and spoken at numerous high-profile men's conferences across North America. Here's what I've learned: Meaningful ministry to men *cannot* evolve from grass-roots efforts. For too long we have ignored the senior pastor and asked lay leaders to move the mountain.

I believe that men's ministry (pancake breakfasts, camping trips, PK rallies, ISI events, and the like) can easily be run by lay leaders. However, that is not ministry to men; it is men's ministry. And there is a big difference.

I have yet to see a truly effective ministry to men where the senior pastor was not fully involved and in charge. In communicating this point, I want to be careful not to take anything away from the talented lay leaders across the country who are doing an incredible job in the area of men's ministry. Rather, what I would like to focus on is the difference between efficiency and effectiveness.

If ministry to men is defined as bringing men into meaningful relationship with God and developing them into fully devoted followers of Christ who can make a difference in their world, then churches need to move from an event-led ministry into a more intentional, pastor-led ministry. Even in large churches where there are several levels of management, ministry to men should report directly to the senior pastor. This sends a strong message to the whole church about priorities.

Perhaps, just as important is identifying and equipping trustworthy men to be part of the discipling process. In 2 Timothy 2:2, Paul lays out the plan: "The things which you have heard from me in the presence of many witnesses, entrust these to faithful men who will be able to teach others also" (TLB). Let's establish a structure for that strategy.

PICKING YOUR LEADERS

Consider God's order here on planet earth. It flows from God the Father, to Jesus the Son, to the man as the spiritual head of the family, to his wife, and ultimately to their children. Where, in that order, is the first place the church can make an impact? Obviously, it's with the man. But look at your calendar and annual budget. There's a good chance you'll see that there's much greater investment in youth and women's ministries than on ministry to men. It seems that we have our ministry priorities out of order.

If you agree, here are some suggestions on how you can move forward. Prayerfully consider two or three, or perhaps in larger churches, as many as eight to ten men you believe possess a level of maturity and a desire to be involved in ministry to men. Call each man individually and ask him if he would consider helping you manage the most important ministry in the church. Invite him into your office for a one-on-one interview.

Treat the interview the way you would if you were hiring an executive staff member. This communicates a level of importance that will stimulate your candidates. Share your passion for ministry, and let them know how you think this is going to impact the church. Give each man a strong vision, and then ask him if he will join the first string.

Once you have your first string in place, ask this group of men to prayerfully consider a list of ten to twenty (depending upon church size) additional men who they believe carry a passion for ministry to men and have the spiritual maturity to join the next level. Let them know you will be making your own list of candidates as well. Then get your core team together and prayerfully and honestly review these candidates, agreeing on the men you want to invite to the next level.

Use the same formal interview process as before. Again, the idea here is to plant the vision—let them sense your passion as their pastor. You now have a small group of men you can begin calling on for help, and a second level to assist in carrying out the day-to-day management of your new ministry. Together you may want to come up with a name like Men's Ministry Council, or some other clever means of identification, that will give each team member a sense of being part of something special.

DISCIPLE YOUR LEADERS

John Maxwell has said, "We teach what we know but reproduce who we are."[1] That parallels another quotable truth, "At the end of the day, our ministry is only as good as the hands that extend it." Your goal with your leadership team is to help them become, to each other first, what they expect to produce in those they will be serving. In other words, practice discipling each other.

Make a concerted effort to meet, at least weekly, with these leaders with a specific agenda in mind:

- Go through a structured learning system to help these leaders grow spiritually and in their understanding of leadership.
- Carve out time for prayer and encouragement—get to know and minister to their areas of struggle.
- Model transparency—they need to see it in you first.

- Have the difficult conversations with men who are lagging. Ask them to step back in order to grow more before assuming a leadership role.
- Discover the weaknesses and strengths of your team.
- Bring strong training resources geared toward developing good group facilitation. On Target Ministries has recently invested a great deal of time and resources, creating and launching a solid video curriculum for this purpose.
- Develop a plan together, laying out strategies for at least the next year in reaching and discipling men.

LEARNING FROM THE PAST

As you plan your strategies for growing men, many lessons can be learned from the last few decades of what many call the Men's Ministry Movement. While several high-quality ministries have evolved and the flag has been raised, indicating the importance of ministry to men, we have not had the kind of results we had hoped for. In fact, men in the church may be worse off today than they were when the movement began.

That statement is not meant to be a slam aimed at many fine efforts, but rather, a testimony to the power of our culture to pull men away faster than we are able to engage them in meaningful discipleship. One of the reasons this has happened stems from our unwillingness to strive for and measure the right outcomes. Our tendency to value events and numbers over observable spiritual maturity is at the center of this dilemma.

A word of caution here: Please know I would never say events are bad. Rather, I am saying that we may be *eventing* men to death. In putting all our eggs in the *event* basket, we fail to realize that men are rarely experiencing any life-giving transformation. For sure, well-planned events can be a rich, soul-satisfying experience. However, our failure to move men beyond the *event* and into meaningful, ongoing spiritual development is a significant problem and a lost opportunity.

The question is, why are lives not being transformed? It's not because events are uninspiring. It's also not a lack of truth—we have the best truth since Jesus walked our planet. Rather, it's because we fail to give men what they crave most. *It takes a relational environment for truth to become transformational.*

Most church-sponsored ministries to men are awkward at creating the kind of life-giving relational environments where we can move that truth from life implication to life application.

GROWTH THROUGH RELATIONSHIPS

Our job as pastors and leaders is to cast the vision, gather the right people to move that vision forward, and measure the right outcomes—spiritual growth, not numerical breadth. Men grow most effectively through an ongoing commitment to a small-group system around some sort of carefully chosen curriculum. At On Target Ministries, we are committing our entire future to the development of this idea with new curriculum and facilitation training.

One of the primary reasons men give up on small groups has to do with poor group management or facilitation. If they see a well-organized plan and that leaders have high expectations, the men will feel cared for and loved. It is also important that your leaders are highly trained, encouraged, and appreciated—remember what the great Oswald Chambers said, "God will not do any more through you than you first allow him to do in you."

4

HOW TO GET YOUR PASTOR TO PLAY

(GEOFFREY ROSS HOLTZ)

Geoffrey Ross Holtz, MRel, DD, has been the senior pastor of The Summit (an Evangelical Free Church) since 1987. He was recognized as NCMM's Pastor of the Year for 2014. This chapter is an excerpt from his new book, *Are You in the Game or in the Way? The Question for Pastors and Men's Ministry Leaders*. For more information, visit rossholtz.com.

Robert Lewis says the major obstacle to getting a ministry for men started in a local church is the senior pastor. Having been a senior pastor for over forty years now, I can confirm that is undeniably true. I learned that truth firsthand.

About fifteen years ago, a fellow named Brad Stewart was a new member at our church. He came into my office one day and said, "Pastor, we need to get a ministry for men started."

"Get out of my office," I said. "Go away and leave me alone. We have men, and we have ministry; hence, we already have a ministry for men."

I didn't really say that, but that was what I was thinking. Who was he to come into my playground and tell me how this game was to be played? I knew we didn't have an effective men's ministry, but I didn't appreciate him pointing out the obvious. If there was a need for an expanded ministry, I'd be the one telling him what needed to be done. This was my playground, my ball, my game, and I had been doing it a long time. (Yeah, I know, despite our high calling, pastors can be jerks. For the uninitiated, this is called territorialism—or sin, for short.)

Who was he indeed? Well, he was a man on a mission from God, speaking God's plan into our church ministry. He was a man who had a heart for men's souls and lives. So instead of saying what I was thinking, I said, "Okay, Brad, let's get to know each other, pray about this, and start planning." I can be a jerk, but I'm not stupid.

Thus, began a long partnership and friendship, which launched a fruitful ministry to men. Along the way, we learned some important things about starting and maintaining a ministry for men. Since most men's ministries are *not* started by pastors, with some notable exceptions, this is written to guys like Brad who have a burning in their souls to impact the men in their church and community. If this describes you, let me tell you what we learned about overcoming your major obstacle—the senior pastor.

CONSIDER HIS POSITION

Join with the pastor before you ask the pastor to join with you. In evangelical Christianity, we don't consider every word spoken by the pastor to be ex cathedra; that is, we don't believe his words are infallible and absolute truth. We do, however, believe he is the one God has put in place to be the head servant to that one particular flock. Your pastor is accountable to his congregation, to his denominational leaders, and, of course, to God.

Furthermore, he generally has given flesh and blood for this church and has more than a vested interest—it is his life. If you are going to start a ministry within his area of responsibility, you must realize the tension this is going to cause.

The church are his people. Well, actually, they are God's, but God has put this man in an anointed position to oversee this flock. Ultimately, these men will come under your authority also, but that doesn't take them out of his flock. Don't steal these sheep! Don't try to create your own sub-flock. You must consider that he, being human and therefore sinful, may feel as if that is exactly what you are doing. This is the tension you are working under.

Your pastor needs to feel as if you are a part of his ministry before you ask him to be a part of yours. Join his support team, or counsel of leaders, and get comfortable working within his sphere. Participate in the leadership of the church before you branch out into a new area.

Remember, your pastor is going to give an account for what takes place in the church, and that includes responsibility for you. I want to say this in the strongest possible terms: If you don't recognize you are a man under authority, or if you can't lead under that authority, then you are not the man to be leading a ministry.

INCLUDE HIM IN YOUR PLANNING

In our case, Brad turned out to be much better at planning than me. As a US Navy veteran, his training and experience made him a natural at building the foundation and strategizing the development of this ministry. But you can bet I wanted to see his plans and strategies before he began implementing them. In my experience, most pastors don't want to micromanage, but we *really* don't want to have to dig ourselves out of a hole excavated by someone else.

Anyone who has been in the pastorate more than a few minutes knows it is harder to correct a ministry gone awry than to start from scratch and build a new solid foundation. So draw up your goals and make your plans, but include your pastor in the foundation building. You may have great vision and a brilliant strategy, but if he doesn't feel he has input into them, you are going to have a tough time making them work.

STAY IN CONSTANT COMMUNICATION WITH HIM

A ministry to men in the local church must not be—or even *feel* like—a parachurch organization. Let's face the facts. If you are a guy who feels called to start a ministry to men, you undoubtedly have a strong personality to go with that. And so does your pastor. That is going to create tension. And it should. There is an old saying that if two men agree completely on everything, one of them is unnecessary.

If God put it in your heart to start such a ministry, he has given you ideas and goals that are necessarily somewhat different than what your pastor has in mind. In this case, two heads are better than one. But you need to make sure the left hand knows what the right hand is doing. Be intentional about communicating what you feel God wants you to do.

It is not sufficient for you to file your business plan and then copy your pastor on what you are doing. He needs to know not only what you are doing, but what you are thinking. Time consuming, to be sure, frustrating, without a doubt, and bothersome at times—but absolutely necessary. You really do need him to be your advocate. You need him to support what you are trying to accomplish.

I know of nothing that will foul a ministry faster than the ministry leader and the senior pastor not being on the same page. And nothing will protect that from happening more profoundly than being in regular communication.

LISTEN TO HIM

Yes, I know, your pastor is not the gatekeeper of all wisdom. But he probably has been around the block a few times and has learned some things along the way. He certainly does not have all the answers, but hey, that's why he has you, hmmm? And, unfortunately for him and you, you don't have all the answers either, or you'd be in holding all the keys. Am I right?

The Bible teaches there is wisdom in the counsel of faithful men. Your pastor is familiar with the dynamics surrounding your church. He has knowledge of things that, I can assure you, you don't. He is an asset to your ministry. Use him. Tell him what God is telling you, then listen to what God is saying through him to you. I don't mean just *hear* what he is saying; I mean listen to his words and to his heart. Maybe he isn't Solomon, but now and again there will be real wisdom in his thoughts and ideas. Pay attention.

When all is said and done, your pastor should have—and does have—the final say. You need to trust that God has put him in that role for a reason. So back him up. And don't complain behind his back.

I wish I could say that doing these four things—considering his position, including him in your planning, staying in constant communication, and listening to him—will guarantee your ministry success. Alas, it will not. But it will help you overcome what is said to be your major obstacle in getting started.

I was such an obstacle. These things worked to win me over. Joshua's Men, our ministry for men, became a thriving ministry at The Summit in Enumclaw, Washington. Of course, there were many other things needed to make this ministry a success too. But for that to happen, as you remember, the ministry had to overcome its first obstacle—me.

Section II

SUCCESSFUL MEN'S EVENTS

5

WHY YOU SHOULD TAKE YOUR MEN TO A MEN'S CONFERENCE

(TOM CHESHIRE)

Tom Cheshire is the founder of Relevant Practical Ministry for Men and has been active in discipling men for over twenty years. Learn more at rpmfm.org.

I f you are a senior pastor or men's pastor, then several thoughts may have come to mind as you read the title of this chapter:

- *Been there, done that.*
- *I have too much to do—I can't afford a day away.*
- *I can take care of my guys at my own church.*
- *I'm not sure my guys would want to spend a day at a men's conference.*
- *I thought Promise Keepers was dead.*

I'm here to tell you that the men's conference is alive and well. There are Christian men's conferences offered all around the nation. Some draw dozens and some draw thousands. Regardless of the size or location, Christian men's conferences continue to change the lives of thousands of men every year.

There may be a men's conference in your city or town, or you may have to travel hundreds of miles to attend one. Just do it. Gather your men, and go. There's no better way to build relational capital with your guys.

RELATIONAL CAPITAL

Everyone understands what financial bankruptcy is—you lack the financial capital to pay your debts. But much worse than financial bankruptcy is relational bankruptcy. In the church, we ask men to serve, teach, mow, paint, pound nails, drive the bus, and park cars. We are happy to make withdrawals, but rarely do we make deposits. Eventually men run out of relational capital, and they burn out.

Let's look at relational capital from a slightly different angle. Author Gary Chapman says that a married woman receives deposits in her "love account" when her husband speaks her love language. For example, my wife's love language is "receiving gifts." It took me a while to really understand that while I had properly identified her love language, it really wasn't about the gifts as much as it was about the thought and action it took when I gave her something. Unless I consistently make deposits in her account, I risk getting an "overdraft" notice when I attempt to make a withdrawal.

The men we lead have a similar relational account. Investing a day with your men at a well-organized conference is one of the best ways to make a relational deposit into the accounts of many men at once.

ANNOUNCING, INVITING, AND TRAVELING WITH YOUR MEN

Deposit #1: Make it clear that you, their pastor or leader, will be attending the conference with them. Your announcement affirms that your men are important and that you care about them. Most guys really want to spend time up close with their pastor or men's leader. The men of your church know you are busy; they know you are pulled in a hundred different directions. Your firm commitment tells the men in your leadership team and church that you want to spend time with them, which in turn kindles their enthusiasm for the event.

Deposit #2: If you can, announce the event from the pulpit and ask the men to join you. Do it repeatedly to build enthusiasm. Many, if not all, of your men will hear this as the commander of their battle group calling them to action. Promotion is important, but nothing gets the same results as a pastor calling his men to join him on a road trip.

Deposit #3: Make personal invitations. Call guys. Text them. E-mail them. Get your men's leaders and elder team to help you. Don't forget the guys on the fringe or who are moderately active and who need to turn it up a notch. There's nothing more effective than a phone call or a face-to-face invitation. Even if they can't attend the event, the fact that you personally invited them will deposit a few coins into their relational account.

Deposit #4: Make the sign-up a big deal. Buy a large poster board, and put your pastor and some key names on it so men know they are part of something special. When a man signs up, give a cheer. Take advantage of any early registration discount. Men understand deadlines, and you can use those dates to get that commitment.

Deposit #5: If some men truly cannot afford to go, then make it an opportunity for outreach and team building. You don't have to mention any names, but if you let your team know that a few guys want to attend but are short on cash, don't be surprised when a few godly men step forward and sponsor their fellow sojourners. That kind of interdependence will help all the men come together in unity.

Deposit #6: A week or two before the event, schedule an information session that features some ice breaking and team building. Play "Two Truths and Lie" or some other game. Ask each man to give one expectation he hopes to gain from attending. Take notes so you can follow up later and ask if that expectation was met *and* what unexpected gift they may have received. As the pastor shares and joins in with the men, he will not only increase his relational capital, but it will help all the men gain relational capital with each other.

Deposit #7: Remind your men to stick together throughout the day of the event, being intentional about sharing breakthroughs and observations with each other. As a pastor or men's leader, you're someone the men want to hang out with. If possible, travel in the largest vehicle you can so all the men can be with you. How cool would it be if you had to rent a bus to make that happen? The ability to travel together speaks volumes to your men and gives you the ability not only to speak and encourage them as a whole, but also to have smaller group interaction or one-on-one time with them. If you do a caravan of cars, make a point to stop along the way for fellowship at a man-friendly restaurant.

Deposit #8: Follow up on the way home or within a couple weeks of the event. Perhaps have a few men come up front during a Sunday service and share specific highlights. That will bless the wives, children, and those who didn't attend. And next year you may need two buses!

AT THE EVENT

Most daylong men's rallies begin with check-in and singing. The first time a man hears a room full of baritone and bass voices belting out well-chosen praise songs and hymns can be a life-changing experience. There's power in manly worship. Follow that with a no-holds-barred message that speaks to the heart of men, and every man will be glad he came.

At lunch and breaks, dialogue with the men about what they are learning, as well as sharing your own new insights. It's okay to admit that you're still growing in your faith too.

Traveling home or at a planned follow-up session, share how God moved and ask your men to share a few key takeaways from their day. Listen intently to show you care and to find out how you might invest in each man going forward. As they share what God revealed to them at the conference, the value of your investment will become clear. Plus, you'll open a new window into their lives.

Now that you know your men better (and they know one another better), expect dividends to continue being deposited into their relational accounts for months afterward. The men who spent the day with you, traveled with you, worshiped with you, and broke bread with you will value that deeper bond for years to come. Shared experiences can do that.

Expect God to do great things at the conference. You may very well trace one man's victory over an addiction or relational crisis to that mountaintop day. Forever friendships will be formed. Best of all, this group of men may see you in a whole new light, not only as their pastor, but as their brother. They'll come to realize you really do care for their souls—that is the biggest deposit of all!

A TRUE STORY ABOUT ONE MAN

There was a man who knew he was hiding and living a double life. He knew he was not honoring God. Week after week, he sat in the pews of his church, convicted, trapped, and knowing he needed to come clean. One Sunday his pastor asked him to join him and the other men at a men's conference. The mere invitation prompted the man to repent.

Two weeks before that conference, the man's sins were revealed to his wife and coworkers, and he came and confessed them to his pastor. Two weeks later, he boarded a bus with fifty other men. He was encouraged on the bus, moved to repentance at the conference, and he testified and celebrated with the men on the way home. His marriage began to heal as his wife forgave him. He met a man on the bus who would disciple him for years to come. Eventually, God called that man into full-time vocational ministry to be a resource to the local church and to encourage and equip them to invest in their men.

If you haven't guessed, the man in that story is me. And it all started by one man inviting me to join him at a men's conference.

6

MARKETING CHRISTIAN EVENTS TO YOUR COMMUNITY

(DR. JIM GRASSI)

Dr. Jim Grassi, best-selling author and international speaker, and his Men's Ministry Catalyst (MMC) team have a host of valuable and timely resources to assist churches and men's organizations in how to pray, plan, execute, market, and evaluate ministry to men. Visit mensministrycatalyst.org for more information. Contact MMC today for a free gift.

Y ou can have the most eloquent of speakers, a great prayer team, amazing program planning, and a sound business strategy for your event, but if you don't have an effective marketing plan to reach the men within your fellowship and those you wish to be in your church, your efforts are in vain.

In churches, Christian ministries, and organizations, the ultimate purpose of marketing is to bring people to the saving knowledge of Jesus Christ and the character of Christ through programs, services, and ministry opportunities. Romans 10:13–14 confirms, "'Everyone who calls on the name of the Lord will be saved.' How, then, can they call on the one they have not believed in? And how can they believe in the one of whom they have not heard? And how can they hear without someone preaching to them?"

Marketing events and activities doesn't happen by accident; they require careful planning. But it doesn't have to be complex and time consuming. The foundation is basic and simple. It begins with two clarifying questions: What is the purpose of the event? And who do you want to attend the event?

WHAT IS THE PURPOSE OF THE EVENT?

Is the primary purpose of the event to promote fellowship within segments of the current congregation? Is your purpose the teaching or the training of a current segment of the church (parents, men, or women)? Is the purpose to introduce the church to the community? Fundamentally, are you doing the event to encourage the members of the church or is it an outreach program? If you don't have a specific purpose in mind for having the event, then why go through the effort and expense?

WHO DO YOU WANT TO ATTEND THE EVENT?

In other words, identify your target audience. Be specific. Is it men? Women? Youth? Don't try to be all things to all people. Using the shotgun approach to marketing, in which you spray information everywhere in hopes of attracting someone, is costly, time consuming, and ineffective. Different audiences respond to different kinds of imagery and messaging. For example, if you're marketing a men's event, it's not a good idea to show pictures of men hugging and crying. Most men are repelled by this type of imagery.

MARKETING PRINCIPLES

With wisdom and discernment, event planners should take full advantage of proven marketing principles to promote Christian events, activities, and programs:

1. The more support you have, the more support you get. When the senior pastor, staff, and lay leadership actively support an event or activity, others (the congregation and members) get behind it and support it too. When there is only nominal staff support, only few join the movement.

2. The more people involved, the more people get involved. Planning, organizing, and marketing an event or activity with one or two persons generally doesn't produce good results. But a well-organized team will multiply the reach and impact.

3. Wants and interests are a springboard to meeting needs. Men are drawn to activities that have a specific theme or topic. Hunting and fishing. Motorcycles. Camping. Archery. Basketball. Woodworking. Model railroading. Father-and-son events. Stay away from generic events in an attempt to attract everyone under the sun. Consider the unique interests of your community or an unreached target audience.

4. People are attracted to successful and well-known personalities. If your event has a sports theme, bring in a Christian athlete. Well-known guest speakers are a proven draw that will gain attention from the community at large.

5. When you catch people's attention, you get people's attention. Use "attention getters" that surprise and delight. It's just like fishing. When you use the right bait in the right way, the fish are attracted and bite.

6. People, especially men and growing boys, are attracted to food. To keep guys coming back, don't skimp on the quality or quantity of food. Become known as the church that has good grub.

7. People like to get free gifts and prizes. Door prizes can attract participation, especially if you publicize a variety of prizes with high appeal to your target audience.

8. Schedule events and activities when it is convenient for people to attend. Timing is critical. Coordinate with community and school calendars to avoid scheduling conflicts with other local, regional, or national events. Also, don't forget to take into consideration the time and the season: hunting and fishing seasons, vacations, holidays, and the like.

9. The easiest way to double attendance is "each one bring one." Posters, flyers, radio, television, and newspaper announcements are good ways to market events, and they should be

used. But nothing beats a personal invitation. Equip your guys with well-designed printed invitations they can use with friend, neighbors, and colleagues.

10. People forget, so remind them. Get folks to write it down on their calendars. Send out e-mails. Splash details across your church website. Postcards have good information, but they're not personal, they're expensive to print and mail, and they can arrive too early or too late. The best reminder may be a phone call a day or two before the event.

11. Sell tickets. If you want men to commit to your event, charge admission. It doesn't have to be a lot. Even a small fee of five or ten dollars will cause a man to place a high value on the event because he paid to get in. Offer scholarships to anyone who can't afford to attend. And even if admission is free, print tickets with a price on the face. Scarcity and dollar value cause men to show up.

WORKING WITH OTHERS

Identify other groups, churches, and businesses that may join you in promoting and attending your event. Communicate the value of the event to the entire community. Create win-win-win scenarios. Ask specifically for support and involvement from:

- Sports clubs (fishing, hunting, archery, camping)
- Ministerial groups or pastoral associations
- Church ministry groups (men's, women's, youth, adult classes, home groups)
- Christian clubs and organizations
- Christian businesses
- Sporting goods stores
- Sports bars (yes, this may be a good place to distribute information.)
- Youth organizations (FCA, Young Life, Youth for Christ, Campus Crusade)

MARKETING AND THE MEDIA

Each media outlet has a unique way of getting information to the public. Take full advantage of any church members who have professional or personal connections with members of the media, such as:

- News columns
- Community interest or "perspective" features
- Editorials
- Club and organization newsletters
- Community calendars
- Free newspapers looking for local interest stories
- Church page/religion section
- Letters to the editor (one of the most read sections of the paper).
- Paid advertising (often discounted for nonprofits)
- Local radio stations featuring community calendars, PSAs, and talk shows
- Local Christian stations that can reach an eager audience
- Local television stations, which cover events from a unique angle

Increase your chances of media coverage with a well-written press release or by making intentional connections with a reporter or staff writer. Assign a well-spoken member of your team to pursue different public relations opportunities.

MARKETING WITH WRITTEN/VISUAL MATERIALS

The key to visual materials is impact—attracting immediate attention so the viewer can quickly absorb details. Because of size and space limitations, keep information short and to the point. If possible, provide a printed takeaway (brochure, card, or tear-off reminder). Here are some ideas:

- Tickets with a dollar value printed on the face (even if there is no charge for the event)

- Flyers with and without tear-off tabs
- Posters with and without information pockets
- Bulletin inserts
- Bulletin boards with and without information pockets
- Post-card invitations and reminders
- Banners
- Personal letters with tickets

Consider using discount coupons in newspapers or local magazines. Some of the best results have come from placing ads in weekly community handouts like "Money Savers" or "The Nickel's Worth" in the sports section. Lastly, try showing video clips at meetings and services—make these exciting and dynamic.

DETAILS AND DEADLINES

Develop your promo plan early—months in advance. Media outlets and printers often have long lead times. Even promoting your event within your church requires you to think ahead. A bulletin insert or a mini-drama before the congregation will probably require approval from church leadership and planning from your creative arts ministry team.

LAST BUT NOT LEAST

Cover every event in prayer. This is a powerful marketing tool available only to believers. Use it. Put a prayer team together that is committed to pray individually and in groups. Start every planning meeting in prayer. Ask God to open doors to the message he wants to bring to your community and to the world. Marketing matters, but prayer is of vital importance.

7

TEN SECRETS TO A
GREAT MEN'S NIGHT

(TRUETT WAYNE POOL JR.)

Truett Wayne Pool Jr. is founder of The MENistry, which assists churches in starting or growing their ministry to men. Truett is also the director of men's ministries at Memorial Baptist Church in Spring, Texas, and speaks nationally on men's issues. He can be contacted at waynepool@mbchouston.org.

I have put together and organized a plethora of men's nights, and each time I learn something new. It takes planning, organization, and a lot of attention to detail. It takes a dedicated team of mostly volunteers. And it takes a bit of surrender and trust. One of the biggest truths about any men's event is that no matter how well we prepare, there will still be some unexpected bumps along the road. We need to trust God has the ability and power to turn any blunders or calamities into good. Let me assure you: he does.

Whether it's a huge blowout annual event or a series of smaller targeted events, I encourage you to see the value of each event from several perspectives. That includes team building, leadership training, a chance to help some of your men step out of their comfort zone, evangelism training, positive partnership with other ministries in your church, outreach to pew sitters, outreach to the community, connecting generations, and even, maybe, launching a new dimension to your men's ministry, such as small groups or a handyman ministry.

Notice I didn't include fundraising in this list. Certainly, men newly committed to the mission of the church will dig deeper into their pockets for the collection plate over future months, but asking for money beyond covering the cost of the event should almost never be the goal of a men's night. Below are ten key elements that should be in place before your men's event begins.

1. PRAYER

While it sounds like a Christian cliché, prayer should be item number one on your to-do list. Inviting God's involvement in every part of the event is crucial. Start by praying for the type of event you wish to have, the speaker God wants to use, and the volunteers who will be helping put this night together.

Go with some men to the facility you will be using a couple of days prior to the start of the event and pray over the space. Pray God's presence will be felt during the men's night. Pray the men will have an open heart. Pray over every chair and pew. Take time again with your team on the day of the event. Pray that men's lives will be affected and that those who do not know Jesus as their personal Lord and Savior will be saved. The night can be fun *and* meaningful.

2. TEAM

Don't go it alone. Recruit men who are excited about leading and share the vision for the type of night you are creating. Men's nights have many moving parts, so put different guys in charge of areas based on their gifts and strengths. Make sure each team member is clear about his responsibilities. Give each man personal ownership. While the leader is still responsible for everything, a good team can make or break the entire event.

3. BUDGET

Establish your total budget early for food, speakers, door prizes, and everything else, and then slide dollars from one category to another depending on the focus of the event. Don't necessarily stick rigidly to the same budget as the previous event. Selling tickets and encouraging men to buy an extra ticket with the intention of inviting a friend is an excellent way to recoup some of the costs. In fact, men who purchase tickets are more likely to attend than those who have no investment.

4. STYLE OR THEME

This is a men's night. Make the space look manly. Make it feel comfortable. Most churches are designed with women in mind. Make this night all about the men. No girly colors. Have hunting and fishing equipment around the room, or use sporting equipment for centerpieces. Yes, I said *centerpieces*. Make sure it does not look cheesy.

5. SCHEDULE

Establish a schedule and do your best to stick to it. But you must remain somewhat flexible because invariably things will crop up that are out of your control. Give every member of your team a small printed schedule, especially those who need to hit their marks in a timely manner. Men like predictability. If you do not begin and end on time, the men will not come back for your next event.

6. PROMOTION

Job one is to get support from your pastor. This assures you can promote within the church through bulletins, flyers, and pulpit announcements. Promoting outside the church and reaching unchurched men can be challenging. Equipping your men to hand out well-designed invitations is typically more effective than mass mailings that get tossed in the trash with the junk mail. Social media works with just about all ages these days. Probably the most important strategy is to get your men excited. Promote a mentality of "each one reach one."

7. SPEAKER

Pay for a big name, hoping for a big draw. Or bring in a midrange speaker who has reputable endorsements. Or have your own pastor speak on a topic critical to men that would never make it to a weekend sermon. Mix up your speaker selection over several men's events. Sometimes choose a speaker with a local connection. You can also attract a crowd based on the topic being covered, rather than on the notoriety of the speaker. That topic could be coaching, fathering, balancing work and home, why men hate church, or being a better husband. Sometimes choose a topic that may not have universal appeal, but will draw a select group of enthusiasts, such as hunting, woodworking, music, cars, motorcycles, or creativity. Every event doesn't have to appeal to every guy.

Utilize the men in your church. Someone might have a relationship you are unaware of that will help you get a great speaker. Maybe even consider some of the contributors to this book. It is also important to be aware that honorariums often fluctuate based on the size of the crowd, and most speakers will take your budget into consideration. Out-of-town speakers may also require travel and hotel expenses, which can quickly add up.

8. FOOD

There are two ways to go about feeding the men. The first way is to have a cooking team, and let them prepare all the food. Having men barbeque will save money and motivate guys who love to cook, but otherwise might be hesitant to get involved.

A second idea is to have the food brought in. On the positive side, there are no men stuck in the kitchen, so everyone is involved in the men's night. On the downside, it's a little more expensive. Either way, you will still need to get the food on the plates efficiently, which takes a small army of volunteers. Decide with your team whether you want to get women involved.

9. DOOR PRIZES

When it comes to door prizes, think manly prizes. I've seen churches give away knives, guns, hunting gear, and much more. The promise of high-dollar quality door prizes makes it easier for your men to invite their friends and neighbors. If you have a limited budget, you might think this is impossible. But a few phone calls can have a big ROI. Many businesses, especially sporting goods stores, will donate items. We recently gave away almost $2,800 worth of prizes and only spent about a hundred and fifty bucks. A single team member took the time and effort to reach out to local businesses. Make sure you recognize those businesses at the event verbally and with signage or on slides, and send a thank-you note. They'll come through for you again next time. In the following weeks, if shoppers intentionally express their gratitude to the store managers, that's a win-win.

10. SALVATION

Let's face it—we don't have these men's nights just for fun and food. The goal is to lead men to Christ and help them grow in their walk, affecting real change in real lives. I tell men at the beginning of the night that they can grab anyone from the men's leadership team at any time for prayer, counsel, or just to talk. There should also be an option at the end of the speaker's message for men to respond. Many will disagree with this, because it might make men uncomfortable. Sometimes that uncomfortable feeling can be God working on their hearts. Have your leadership team ready to witness to men who might want to learn more about a true relationship with Christ. Accepting Jesus as Savior will be the best prize given that night, truly making the night worth all the effort.

EXTRA TIPS

Here are some final tips on how to plan a successful men's night:

- Be sure to have handouts about the church for visitors.
- Get visitor information so you can do follow up. I recommend including space for name, phone number, e-mail, and home address on the back of tickets for the event or prize drawing. Station volunteers at the entryway or have table leaders check to make sure the blanks are mostly filled out, but don't make a big deal about it. Never force a man to give his personal information.
- Have prayer cards and pens at each table, as well as a prayer table where these cards can be turned in. After the event, gather members of your team to pray over these cards. Have

members stationed at the prayer table throughout the night to pray with any men who need it.

- With a display table or on rotating slides, showcase great photos of past events. Men are visual and need to see what's going on—and what they're missing.
- Promote upcoming studies or activities. Play a well-produced video. Have a couple of men give a two-minute testimony on how these opportunities blessed them. Pass around a sign-up sheet or hand out cards requesting more information.
- Have your leadership team wear the same style shirt, preferably with your logo on it. This identifies men who can help and answer questions, and it reflects the brotherhood men crave.
- For posters, prayer cards, tickets, and more, try using websites like Vistaprint or Kinkos. They are reasonably priced and provide you with professional-looking items.

Finally, I know you want things to run like clockwork. But I urge you not to judge your event too harshly. You may think the food was cold and the audience didn't connect with the speaker. The microphone failed. The snow kept dozens of guys from coming. And none of the five men you had been praying for and personally invited showed up. I've learned to smile while cleaning up after those kinds of events. Almost always—a few weeks later—reports trickle in of how God moved mightily during that evening despite our flawed best efforts.

8

WHAT'S NEXT? CAPTURING THE MOMENTUM FROM A BIG EVENT

(DAVE WERTHEIM)

Dave Wertheim is the founder and president of Men U for Transformed Lives, and a Man in the Mirror faculty trainer. He is the author of *Men U: Courses for a Transformed Life* and *Men U: Advanced Courses for a Transformed Life*. Find out more at davewertheim.com.

I was the new men's ministry director at our church. My team and I had just organized a successful men's retreat. By all accounts, the speaker, music, venue, food, small-group time, and camaraderie met every expectation. At the end of the retreat, many men who had been moved by the experience asked how they could maintain the mountaintop experience. "Well guys, we have men's small groups starting in the fall," I said. That was four months away. As you can imagine, all the energy of that retreat quickly dissipated.

I learned a valuable lesson that sunny May afternoon: Our retreat team had worked hard to build momentum, but we squandered it because we had no plan to capture it. Many churches are skilled at gathering men for events but fail to transition those men into ongoing disciple-making relationships.

The key to getting men into these relationships is to give them an appropriate, believable next step. And then another. And then another. That's how they will become fully integrated into your church and the discipleship process. For every event you organize (big or small), as part of the planning process, consider the opportunities you will offer the men. *Always show men the right next step.*

Man in the Mirror has been discipling men and developing tools for leaders for more than thirty years. After working with more than twenty-five hundred churches, we've identified some best practices that capture momentum from events. Here are seven tips for capturing momentum.[1]

1. MAKE THE FOLLOW-UP FIT THE EVENT

If you have a men's retreat or breakfast with a speaker who has written a book, a logical next step is to form new groups that will read, study, and apply the book together. Or organize a service day for a group of men and help do maintenance and repair on a widow's home. Possible follow-up opportunities could be to create an ongoing service ministry team or consider a short-term mission trip with those same guys.

2. RIGHTSIZE THE COMMITMENT YOU ARE ASKING FOR

Make sure the commitment is something that a man can see himself doing. It has to be a believable next step and something he can get excited about. If the next step seems too hard, is too big a commitment, or is too weird or uncomfortable, you'll encounter resistance. For example, you may be personally excited to do an in-depth study of Isaiah or the book of Revelation, but is a nine-month detailed study the right next step for most guys? I've led numerous studies on these books, which are rich with God's Word, but that was the right next step for the small group I was leading at the time. Rightsize the commitment so it's the right next step for the men you are trying to win at the event.

3. ALWAYS HAVE AN ENDING POINT

Men are reluctant to make an open-ended commitment, so keep the commitment short, no more than four to six weeks at a time. Man in the Mirror uses four- to six-week follow-up materials for every seminar we deliver, because men can see themselves participating in something for a short period of time. If they don't like it, they can gracefully bow out at the end. It's not a lifetime commitment. (Although, when it's done well, men will re-up and continue the small group process when they build connections with the other guys in the group, which is the momentum capture point for the follow-up group.)

4. CHOOSE GOOD "SECOND GEAR" MATERIAL

If you want men to continue with the next step, then it has to be something that is accessible and meets their needs. Use materials that address the issues of the day and cause men to think about biblical guidance and spiritual application. When you evaluate material, ask, Will this meet the needs of the guys I expect to participate? If not, then pick something else.

5. START NEW GROUPS FOR NEW MEN

For a long time, I've had multiple small groups going and would invite guys to join me anytime during the year. It is much harder for a man to join an existing group than it is to join a brand-new group where everyone else is also a newbie. If you are launching a follow-up group, start it fresh so everyone is at the same starting point. You will want to assign a veteran to lead the group to make sure they don't spin off course.

6. HELP MEN TAKE THE NEXT STEP— ON THE SPOT

When I started as a men's ministry director, our church organized gym nights. We'd play basketball, volleyball, and have other games and contests so there was something for everyone. At the end of the night, we announced all our small groups and had sign-up sheets in the back of the gym with the meeting dates, topics of study, locations, and leader's name, and then instructed the men to go sign up. And our response? Zero. Men won't sign up for a group without knowing who else is in the group and who their leader is going to be.

Man in the Mirror has perfected an effective technique to dramatically increase the percentage of men who will take the right next step by getting an onsite commitment. Throughout our seminars, we emphasize the importance of leveraging their time and taking a next step. Toward the end of the seminar, we designate one of the table discussion times to form follow-up groups. We have each leader stand, introduce himself, and share the details about when and where his group will be meeting. We insist that every man in attendance pick one of these groups for the discussion time and physically go sit at that table.

Once there, the men meet each other, exchange contact information, and discuss some prearranged questions. This breaks the ice, and guys get to know the other men who "might be" in this new group. At the end, the discussion leader confirms the date and time of the next meeting. Since the leader has the contact information, he can follow up with each man and encourage him to attend, and answer any questions or concerns he might have.

When churches use this method, we've found more than two-thirds of the men decide to join the group. And many who attend have *never* been in a small group before.

7. THE POWER OF A PERSONAL INVITATION

There's nothing more powerful than the personal invitation.

Train your leaders to reach out to men at events to join them in taking the right next step. Here's an example of a good invitation: "Joe, I attend a great men's group that is studying how to improve our marriages (or parenting or finances), would you like to join me this week? I'll pick you up at Wednesday at six in the morning, and we can go get breakfast afterward."

Do these tips only apply to big events like retreats and breakfasts? No. Proactively identifying the right next step can (and should) be incorporated into *everything* you do. If a man attends your small group, a right next step might be acquiring or practicing a spiritual discipline (along with coming back the following week). Or perhaps identifying his spiritual giftedness or passion, and helping him put it into action.

Does this only apply to men's-only events? No. There are far more opportunities through your all-church events (picnics, Sunday school, potlucks, or anything else your church puts on). Design next-step opportunities and work with your church allies to set aside a few minutes to rally the men and promote your next men's ministry event or circulate among the crowd, make some new friends, and hand out flyers. For example, if your church has a fall harvest festival, arrange to have something fun for dads at the event (like a putting green), and organize a golf scramble a few weeks after. Or have a basketball hoop or mini-hoop setup for guys to show off their prowess and have tickets available for a family night at your local pro or college basketball arena.

NOW WHAT?

What's your right next step after reading this chapter? Why not decide today that you will look at your upcoming church events and design a right next step for the men in attendance? Get together with your planning team, and make it happen. See how easy this is?

Section III

ONE-ON-ONE DISCIPLE-MAKING

9

DISCERNMENT AND DISCIPLESHIP

(KENNY LUCK)

Kenny Luck is the leadership pastor at Crossline Church in Laguna Hills, California. He was previously the men's pastor at Saddleback Church in Lake Forest, California. He is also the founder and president of Every Man Ministries, which helps churches worldwide develop and grow healthy men's communities with the goal to end child abuse, fatherlessness, and protect women and children. He has authored and coauthored twenty-one books, including *Every Man, God's Man*, and *Sleeping Giant*.

The author of Proverbs reminds us, "Watch over your heart with all diligence, for from it flow the springs of life" (Proverbs 4:23 NASB). One of the tools cardiologists depend on is a heart scan. Magnetic resonance imaging (MRI) or computed tomography (CT) scans allow both patient and doctor to see small structures or blockages, peer into valves and chambers, assess the overall structure and shape of the heart, and look directly at the coronary arteries feeding into the heart.

Jesus did the same thing, spiritually speaking. He could see right through the masks, motives, and self-protecting tactics of a man, looking right into his heart. Jesus could see where the spiritual or emotional blockages were clogging his ability to believe. He could peer into the valves and chambers of his experiences, assess the overall structure of the character these experiences created, and look directly at the truths or lies presently feeding into his beliefs about God's plan for his life.

Like an MRI, Jesus was noninvasive. He took pictures. He helped people see a true image of themselves—and clearly presented the problem. Then he offered himself and his way as the solution. Think of Jesus' interactions with the woman at the well (John 4), the rich young ruler (Matthew 19:21–22), the Pharisees (Mark 7:5–8), and Martha (Luke 10:38–42). Each of these "patients" had a choice: accept the diagnosis and be healed, or reject it and remain sick; to pursue spiritual health now, or put it off for later.

As a disciple maker, Jesus wants to give you *his* ability to see past the externals straight into a man's heart. This is called *discernment*. Here is a biblical nonnegotiable when you disciple another man: "And this is my prayer: that your love may abound more and more in knowledge and depth of insight, so that you may be able to discern what is best and may be pure and blameless until the day of Christ, filled with the fruit of righteousness that comes through Jesus Christ—to the glory and praise of God" (Philippians 1:9–11).

To be loving in a meaningful way toward others requires discernment, which, in turn, requires a good knowledge and understanding of people. A man's gestalt (pronounced *geh-shtalt)* is his core thoughts and experiences, which, when integrated, constitute *who he really is* as opposed to who he is presenting himself to be.

Jesus was great at nailing people's gestalt. He could and would go there *because he loved them deeply*. This is why for God's man there is a clear connection between having a deep, Christlike love for people, and the quantity of insight God gives that man into others.

Anyone who would minister to men should read Matthew 23 with great fear and trembling. The first-century hypocrites Jesus describes with such disdain are still among us today. They do far more damage than good in God's name because their behavior says they love themselves more than they love the people they claim to be trying to guide and helping spiritually. Real discernment of people without Christ-centered love is not possible. Otherwise, we have what is most commonly known as "an agenda"—satan loves those.

A true discipler of men must be guided by a real love for those whom he disciples. That love gives him an ability to see the important stuff, or "discern," what really matters to God, to him, and to his way of thinking. Watch Jesus work. He was neither enamored nor interested in the external "show" or the public presentations of those he mentored. He had no appetite for dealing with symptoms, because he was obligated by love to go after the root causes of another man's bondage. His mission was to enter and redeem hearts, not respond to the disguises, diversions, or denials of reality.

What does Jesus model for those of us who are discipling men? Go after *the real issues that affect an individual's relationship with God and others.* Jesus knew what we all know: people are like icebergs—we only see the tip, but there's a deeper spiritual drama unfolding below the waterline.

Christ had a highly developed heart sonar—a spiritual ultrasound—that was constantly measuring the invisible world of the heart. Jesus took snapshots of men's hearts—and then showed the X-ray. Some embraced the truth and asked to be healed. Others were content to remain in their sickness.

Men are much the same today. They will try to use "head tactics," goofy logic, silence, or dysfunctional reasoning to either justify, defend, divert, excuse, or draw attention away from themselves and their core heart problems. In a man's walk with Jesus, clogged spiritual arteries restricting the work of the Holy Spirit will eventually lead to an episode of the heart that can be fatal to his witness and destroy his walk if left unaddressed.

Every man we disciple is just like us—we all have hurts. Fears. Insecurities. Sin. Mixed motives. Lust. Wounds. Abandonments. Shame. Pride. Loss. Negative emotions. These heart wounds are the places where real pain, pride, or paranoia exist. But they are also the places that offer the greatest potential for spiritual transformation.

When you know how human beings are wired, you know exactly where to probe, what to look for, where to cut, where to attempt removal of a spiritual cancer, and where to take the healing process between a person and God. He gave Samuel some awesome ministry advice when he said: "Do not look at his appearance or at the height of his stature, because I have rejected him; for God sees not as man sees, for man looks at the outward appearance, but the LORD looks at the heart" (1 Samuel 16:7 NASB).

That's what Jesus did with men. You could not be a spiritual Switzerland (as in neutral) and be around Jesus for any length of time. He would go straight to your trigger issue to precipitate a choice. An effective disciple maker will know how to get to a man's heart issues. The biggies would be his:

- Family stuff, both past and present
- Family hurts and losses (if any)
- Relationships
- Current or core struggles
- Core fears
- Biggest hurts
- Wiring as man

These issues don't reveal themselves right away. But once a man feels safe with you and gets comfortable talking about these issues, you'll often get an up-close-and-personal look right into the chambers of his heart. You'll get a crystal-clear picture of his heart and the obstacles that are keeping him from following Christ. This is where Jesus went with men, and this where God wants you to go with men too.

When you love people and care to search out the main issues of their heart with only one agenda—to help them connect better with God and others—you get handed a divine ultrasound that reveals who they really are: their standards, ethics, motives, driving passions, and true gods. Like Jesus, you are called to train yourself to recognize the differences between appearances and reality, public images and private struggles, anger and hurt, pride and fear. God's man, like the God-man, is ever growing in his abilities to scan for good versus bad intentions, right versus wrong agendas, healthy versus unhealthy spiritual patterns, and the vital versus the trivial issues in people's words, behaviors, and thought processes.

But before you can peer into another man's heart, you must allow

Jesus to examine your heart. Study his ways, get his mind from the Scriptures, dialogue with him, ask him for discernment, listen for his voice, and, above all, *respond to his direction for your life*. Only then can you help the lost find their way to him and, ultimately, to find their healing in him. We can't give away Holy Spirit discernment when our own hearts are bound by self-deception.

In the end, it's hard for people to conceal themselves from a discerning God's man. Jesus will strip away our immature and self-protective defenses and replace them with his acceptance and authority. The result? A disciple sees himself and others more clearly. When a man whose fears have been defeated by love approaches another fearful person, there's no need to pretend. That's when they see him—in you. They just can't fake it when Jesus, the seer of hearts, is in the house.

10

FINDING DISCIPLES

(ART HOBBA)

Art Hobba is the founder of Core 300, an executive coach and leadership consultant with Transcende, and the author of *Called to War,* the *Core 300 Trilogy,* and *The Six Stages of Leadership.* He loves walking with his wife and spearfishing, and he can be reached at art.hobba@core300.org.

As a boy in the 1960s, I gathered with my family to watch the NASA astronauts lift off from Cape Canaveral on our black-and-white television. Mercury, Gemini, and Apollo missions had us on pins and needles as the countdown descended. We all knew that, after liftoff, if all went well for the first sixty seconds, the likelihood was that the mission would be a success.

Like those missions, Jesus found success when he prepared for and focused on *the finding* of the men he would call to follow him as disciples. It only makes sense that today, if we follow Christ's process as he identified and engaged the twelve, we will be on solid footing. Then as the discipleship experience unfolds, many things will supernaturally fall into place.

Let us first drill into the word *disciple.* I like the medieval term *liege man,* that describes the relationship between a squire and his knight or a soldier and his captain. Liege is the root of the word *allegiance,* and you become a liege man through a solemn public ceremony, where an inferior willingly kneels before his superior and swears allegiance for a period of time. This allegiance included loyalty of heart and the protection of his lord, his people, and his property. Your life and sword arm, when requested, belonged to your liege lord.

WHAT IS A DISCIPLER?

The immensely important role of the "discipler" is one who is seeking, finding, engaging, and developing another man from a basic follower of Jesus—a disciple in training—into a solid discipler himself. The discipler begins his action phase with the "finding" of that man. Today, because so many potential disciplers fail to seek and recruit new disciples, the system has broken down. This reveals and underscores why the church in the US is ailing, weak, and losing the adherents of the next generation.

Arguably, discipling was the primary ministry of Jesus. Other than the dual Great Commandment of loving God and loving one another, the most singular ministry command from Jesus to us is to "go and make disciples" (Matthew 28:19). Many of the pastors I have talked to about discipleship will admit that being "one to many," the Sunday morning model of church, is ineffective in making disciples. It is vital for teaching and worship, of course, but as Jesus showed us, his primary focus was on building relationship with the twelve.

SEEKING THE DIVINE PROCESS

Jesus spent three years living with, mentoring, and teaching twelve young men. That same model is ours to follow today. As a matter of fact, we should expect any program that has a lasting impact to take that length of time. You can't rush disciple making. That's why our own Core 300 program features a three-year curriculum and sequentially engages and interactively trains disciples in the seminal dimensions of devotion to God, connection and trust within the group, and commitment to their sphere of ministry service as it unfolds.

FINDING THE GUY, STEP ONE: THE CHRISTLIKE MIND-SET

Those of us who are Christ's liege men are called to go out into our world and find, recruit, and disciple (the verb, not the noun) other men to follow Jesus as their liege Lord as well. In my journey, there have been two principles of discipling that have rung true: First, I cannot take a guy to a place of enlightenment, liberty, and ego sacrifice, or into the joys of selfless service, *unless* I have lived there and know the GPS coordinates by heart; and second, that man won't trust me to show him the higher and often paradoxical ways of the Master until I show him my scars, especially the recent open, still-healing ones.

Imagine the astonishment of those simple Galilean fishermen when Jesus said to them, "Take my yoke upon you ... for I am meek and lowly" (Matthew 11:29 KJV). The word he chose for *lowly* meant "an ongoing posture of walking low to the ground." Jesus refers to himself repeatedly as a slave, a person without rights, who gives himself up to another's will.

Scars Are Tattoos with Much Better Stories

The real test of courage is the willingness to confess a weakness in a place where you might be misunderstood. James 5:16 teaches us, "Confess your sins to each other and pray for each other so that you may be healed." The *you* in this verse is not singular, but plural. James was not just writing about the healing of the person who is confessing, but the healing of whoever is being confessed to as well.

Recent neuroscience studies have proven that when one person confesses his or her sin, or shows vulnerability to another in the form of a personal story, pleasing hormones are released in the brain of the listener, creating two things. First, it creates within the person listening an almost compelling desire to reciprocate by confessing something intimate back to the confessor. And second, it creates within the person listening an almost instantaneous bond of trust, attended by a marked increase of respect for the confessor.

How counterintuitive can you get? Do you want to be a great discipler for Jesus? Practice the same Christlike mind-set he did. Be intentional, walking *low to the ground* in heart and in mind. Be vulnerable, unafraid to show your scars, even your recent ones.

FINDING THE GUY, STEP TWO:
EMBRACE THE DISCIPLINE OF PRAYER

Jesus was committed to the regular discipline of extended time alone with his Father in heaven. Most guys I know start to fidget when it comes to prayer, especially praying alone. But you cannot deny that this is what went down with Jesus. He prayed for an entire night, then he went out, and bam!—he picked the twelve. We don't know if the Father paraded the faces of the twelve in front of his Son, but I doubt it. When Jesus chose them, they were in his general neighborhood, within fifteen miles of Nazareth. In fact, some may have been good friends from boyhood, because every year caravans of families took the same north-south road to Jerusalem for the Passover, a community celebration of three weeks or more.

If you are ready to be a discipler, pray for God to bring that guy to you. It may be that you already suspect who it might be. If not, God will place the right guy in your path; have your radar on always. *Expect* your next disciple-in-training to come across your path. Don't discount anyone. Is he too young, loud, or arrogant? Think of the three best friends of Jesus. Is he a questioner? Think of Thomas. Maybe he has an "un-Christian" profession like Matthew the tax collector.

It's All about Attitude

Don't look for education or skill levels; rather, look for heart. Look for the man with an all-in attitude. Get his story, and see if he has experienced a purging crucible or two. Who is his favorite biblical character? Ask him why. His answer will reveal the values and characteristics of a core disciple. Ask him about his dad, or whoever mentored or influenced him the most. Does he have a father-shaped hole in his soul? Maybe revealing your own scar is the story of hope he needs to hear.

How does he face his battles? Just as Jesus faced warfare with the devil in the desert at the onset of his ministry, expect that you and the new disciple will be tested as well. This is why I wrote *Called to War*, a field manual for winning the invisible battles of life. The typical lukewarm churchgoing Christian is not dangerous to the kingdom of darkness, but the fully equipped and trained disciple is. He may not yet be trained, but attitude is everything.

FINDING THE GUY, STEP THREE:
GO MILLENNIAL (AGES SIXTEEN TO THIRTY-SIX)

Last year, the Holy Spirit rebuked me because I had developed a condescending attitude toward my five sons. As adults, I judged them as green, untried, and as having a great deal to learn (from me!). No wonder there was an unspoken gap between us. I had to ask their forgiveness, one at a time, and start to listen and understand each of them to begin to have the right to be heard. So far, I have been on the learning side more than they have, but it is good to be their friend.

Millennials are the largest generation in history, and will be the majority of the working force in three years. I know what you're thinking, *Millennials—me? Are you kidding? I wouldn't have a clue how to begin talking with them—and why would they be interested in an old Boomer like me anyway?*

A good friend, Tim Eldred, leads a global youth ministry called Endeavor, and they are shaking it up, training, and deploying thousands of fifteen- to twenty-one-year-olds worldwide to go out and *do* ministry. His research indicates that none of the original disciples called by Jesus were older than twenty-one; if that is the age group Jesus chose to use to launch the church, then who are we to invent a better way?

Don't discount this generation. If they have issues—and, like every emerging generation for thousands of years, they do—it is mostly the doing of the older generation. These young men, who are also the largest fatherless generation in US history, have wandered away from the church by the millions. It is up to us to find them.

It's time for churched men who have proven their faith by tithing, being faithful to our wives, and attending Bible studies and fun men's events to repent. Our most important work is ahead of us. It is time to obey Jesus and go find and make disciples. This emerging generation is looking for reality. Most of them have rejected the lunacy of evolution and believe in an active God. It is on us to use the latent God-given hunger in the hearts of these young men to begin to build them into liege men for the Lord Jesus.

11

HOW TO DISCIPLE MEN THROUGH MENTORING RELATIONSHIPS

(ROY L. COMSTOCK)

Roy L. Comstock, ThD, is the chairman and CEO of the Christian Mentors Network, a national ministry based in Valencia, California. Roy is author of *Mentoring His Way: Disciple Twelve*, which is based on "Twelve Characteristics of a Godly Life." Contact Roy at roy@christianmentorsnetwork.org or go to christianmentorsnetwork.org.

Most of us already know the importance of mentoring. At the Christian Mentors Network, we've identified four essential steps to the mentoring process: engage, equip, empower, and employ.

ENGAGE MEN IN THE MENTORING PROCESS

Definition of *engage*: to become actively involved in or committed to.

Pray

When I mentored my friend Barry, and we decided that it was time for him to mentor someone else, he said, "I don't know anyone I can mentor." He was a new believer, and the only job he had in the church was on the setup crew on Sunday morning. I suggested that we pray that God would bring a man into his life who was already talking to God about wanting a closer walk with the Lord.

The next Sunday morning, Art, one of the men on the setup crew, started talking to Barry about wanting to go deeper in his relationship with Christ. So Barry asked Art if he would like to get coffee after they were through setting up. Art said yes. Prayer has always been the key to finding men to mentor.

Listen

When God brings a man to you and he starts sharing his need for spiritual growth, do what my friend Dr. Dallas Demmitt, author of *Can You Hear Me Now?*, says, "Shut up and listen to God and to what the man is saying. After he speaks for a little bit, review what he has said to make sure you truly understand what he is saying and, even more importantly, so that he knows you understand what it is that he is saying." When you are sure he desires to go deeper in his walk with the Lord, then invite him to meet with you.

Invite

It amazes me how many men are interested in mentoring when they are invited to meet personally. Most men who come to the realization that they want to go deeper in their faith are struggling with issues they would be uncomfortable revealing in a group setting. If it is a large enough group, they may feel safe attending because they can hide in the crowd. In a small group, however, they feel intimidated for fear someone might call on them or ask them a question they are not ready to answer. A one-on-one invitation alleviates those fears.

EQUIP MEN TO BECOME LOVING, OBEDIENT FOLLOWERS OF CHRIST

Definition of *equip*: to furnish for action; make ready by appropriate provisioning.

Mentor

In your first meeting, share a bit about your own life and then listen carefully. Be a friend. Don't have all the answers. Don't dig too deep too soon. Volunteer how God has worked in and through your own life experiences. Tell him how you dealt with certain issues through God's Word and by the direction of the Holy Spirit.

During the mentoring process, allow the mentee to take his time so he can build trust and feel safe enough to eventually share his secrets. He will soon discover he has access to forgiveness without judgment. Once a man knows he is forgiven, heart transformation takes place. But it all starts with a simple invitation.

Exemplify

Any man you mentor should see the fruit of the Holy Spirit in your life and perhaps realize what is missing in his own life. Exemplify the love of Christ in all you do and say. This is not something you can fake. Spend time with the Lord and his Word daily to make sure your own life is right with God in every way. Remember that the fruit of the Spirit is love. We must continue to give control of our life to the Holy Spirit in order to exemplify his love.

Disciple

Mentoring is all about discipling men one-on-one, life on life. In any mentoring relationship, including discipleship among Christians, this means following a specific track that is replicable, personal, and has value and application. We disciple with the Christian Mentors Network curriculum *Mentoring His Way: Disciple Twelve*, which is based on "Twelve Characteristics of a Godly Life." This is a mentoring process that you can learn and pass on to others.

An important aspect of mentoring is teaching your disciples how to become obedient followers of Christ. We are told this in the Great Commission: "Teaching these new disciples to obey all the commands I have given you" (Matthew 28:19).

To change a man's character and behavior, we must first change the way he thinks. The process of transformation, in becoming an obedient follower of Jesus, all starts with our thoughts. Proverbs 23:7 says, "For as he thinks in his heart, so is he" (NKJV). What a man thinks about becomes his values, his values determine his character, and he acts out his character through his behavior.

The mentoring process helps a man see himself the way God sees him. It helps him discover, or in some cases rediscover, his identity in Christ. When a man truly understands who he is in Christ, it changes his behavior. Mentoring is about heart transformation, not behavior modification.

EMPOWER MEN TO RELY ON THE WORD OF GOD AND THE HOLY SPIRIT

Definition of *empower*: to give official authority or legal power.

God's Word

Our entire mentoring process is centered on God's Word. That is why it's so effective in transforming the hearts of those involved, empowering us to become Christlike. The writer of Hebrews tells us this:

> For the word of God is living and active and full of power [making it operative, energizing, and effective]. It is sharper than any two-edged sword, penetrating as far as the division of the soul and spirit [the completeness of a person], and of both joints and marrow [the deepest parts of our nature], exposing and judging the very thoughts and intentions of the heart. (Hebrews 4:12 AMP)

Holy Spirit

The ultimate source of power and our change agent for living as citizens of heaven is the Holy Spirit. Galatians 5:16 promises, "I say then: Walk in the Spirit, and you shall not fulfill the lust of the flesh" (NKJV).

The Holy Spirit leads us into all truth and confirms Jesus' teaching. Jesus said, "All this I have spoken while still with you. But the Advocate, the Holy Spirit, whom the Father will send in my name, will teach you all things and will remind you of everything I have said to you." (John 14:25–26). That is why our mentoring process includes Scripture memory. The Holy Spirit will bring Scripture to our remembrance when we need it, but only if we have previously taken it to heart.

As a believer, you are controlled and empowered by the Holy Spirit, which allows you to reflect the likeness of Christ to the world around you. Those who choose to emulate you will emulate Christ, who is exemplified through you by the Holy Spirit's power. Paul said it best in 1 Corinthians 11:1: "Imitate me, just as I also imitate Christ" (NKJV).

EMPLOY MEN IN THE ACTIVITY OF MENTORING OTHER MEN

Definition of *employ*: to devote to or direct toward a particular activity or person.

Replication

One of the most powerful results of the one-on-one mentoring process is that it produces mentors. Do you remember what Paul said to Timothy, one of his mentees? He wrote, "And the things that you have heard from me among many witnesses, commit these to faithful men who will be able to teach others also" (2 Timothy 2:2 NKJV).

Many in the church talk about their goal of "exponential growth." Whether it is in numbers or in the hearts of men, is there a better way to grow your ministry than to do it the way Paul did it? Or, for that matter, the way Jesus did it?

Continuation

Can you imagine what would happen if every believer decided to make it his mission to mentor twelve others in his lifetime, and then to teach those mentees to do the same thing with a new generation of mentees? When Jesus told us to make disciples, did he put a limit on it? Do you believe he indicated that after we mentored one person, it was okay to stop?

Relationship

Recently, we conducted a survey among some of the men who were mentored in Arizona. The number one reason men wanted to be mentored was to have a more spiritually mature man walk with them and teach them how to live the Christian life, according to what the Bible taught. The reason most gave for following through and going on to mentor others was because of the lasting relationships that were developed during their own mentoring process.

Men realize that having a mature believer they can go to for prayer and encouragement at any time is gratifying, reassuring, and valuable. Experiencing the life transformation that takes place in the man you mentor gives a sense of purpose and significance you may have never known previously. Few things come as close as watching your mentees go from being ordinary Christian men to victorious warriors for Christ. God wins in situations that look hopeless. Mentors and mentees often develop deep relationships that last a lifetime.

12

HOW TO LISTEN
TO MEN

(ROY BALDWIN)

Roy Baldwin is director at Monadnock Bible Conference and former director of parenting and youth for Focus on the Family. He has worked for more than two decades with at-risk youth. You can reach Roy at roylbaldwin@gmail.com and monadnockbible.org.

Like most guys, I think I'm a pretty good husband. Then one day my wife came to me and unloaded. It turns out, I had completely failed to listen to her. I missed the mark because I only saw my needs and expectations, not hers. Now, you might ask, "What does this have to do with leading men?" The answer is because we do the same thing to other men. Instead of listening and responding, we lecture and fix.

Over the years, I have learned some principles that have produced some amazing benefits in the men who come to our camp and conference center in New England. I've boiled the principles down to a simple acrostic: LISTEN. It reminds me that the key to leading and loving well is to listen well, both to God and to others. If you long to lead men, then you need to LISTEN.

LOVE

If I speak in the tongues of men or of angels, but do not have love, I am only a resounding gong or a clanging cymbal. (1 Corinthians 13:1)

Researchers use terms such as "emotional connection" or "warmth" when it comes to leadership in the workplace or in the home. When people make an emotional connection, they perform better. When people know you speak and act out of love, they respond accordingly. Here are some applications:

1. Have each man fill out a basic questionnaire to let you get to know him. Having information about his family, career goals, hobbies, and personal history will help you connect and "love" him well.
2. Meet individually or with a small group of men to "touch base" over coffee or food. That speaks volumes about your love and willingness to listen.
3. Ask open-ended questions, making sure not to make it about you, but about them. You have two ears and one mouth—use them accordingly.

INTENTIONAL

Above all, my brothers and sisters, do not swear—not by heaven or by earth or by anything else. All you need to say is a simple "Yes" or "No." Otherwise you will be condemned. (James 5:12)

How purposeful and intentional are you in getting to know those you lead? Too often—and I know I can fall into this trap—I end up talking way too much about myself. Active listening intentionally builds trust; it makes men feel valued. Here are some tips for truly listening and responding to people:

1. Summarizing lets men know you've listened. Say things like, "It sounds to me like ..." or, "If I hear correct you are ..."
2. Being reflective is your ability to be a mirror for someone when it comes to putting his words into feelings. For example, "That sounds like that really hurt you," or, "That must have made you extremely proud."
3. Validation is especially important for men. Most guys beat themselves up daily. If they aren't, others are doing it for them. Men need validation. State things like, "It takes a ton of courage

to be so transparent with me," instead of, "Seriously, why are you making such a mountain out of a molehill?"

SINCERE

Unlike so many, we do not peddle the word of God for profit. On the contrary, in Christ we speak before God with sincerity, as those sent from God. (2 Corinthians 2:17)

Men are looking for leaders who are sharing the hope of the gospel out of a sincere love for them—no other agenda. Scripture commands our authenticity and calls us to a sincere love and faith. We need to be genuine before God and others. People are attracted to those who are authentic. Men especially are repelled by insincerity and hypocrisy.

Here are some key ways to be sincere with men:

1. You cannot give what you do not have. If you want men to be sincere in their faith and love of Christ and each other, then you must model it. Share stories of your own previous and current struggles and how you are working through them.
2. One of the worst things a leader of men can do is act like he already has it all together or has arrived and everyone needs to act like him. Sincerity is your ability to be authentic and invite people into your world—the good, the bad, and the ugly.
3. Don't make everything polished; it will seem like a sales pitch. Instead, be genuine.
4. Integrity is huge. If you behave a certain way at church in front of the men but act a different way on the job, at a football game, or in your home toward your wife or children, you will forfeit your ability to reach them.
5. The Latin root for the word *courage* is *cor*, meaning "heart." To be sincere will require you to lead men with your heart, which will require courage to be transparent and authentic.

TIME

My dear brothers and sisters, take note of this: Everyone should be quick to listen, slow to speak and slow to become angry. (James 1:19)

You cannot listen to God or others without slowing down and making an investment of time. Busyness isn't ministry. It takes time to know, to love, and to respond accordingly. One of the biggest ways to leverage time is to know felt needs.

What's a felt need? A felt need is a mixture of expectations, priorities, and pain points of the men you are hoping to lead. Addressing their felt needs makes your ministry relevant to their lives, and men will suddenly make time for what you provide. Here are some practical steps:

1. Your quiet time with God is critical to your health and the health of those you lead. No one modeled this better than Christ: "Very early in the morning, while it was still dark, Jesus got up, left the house and went off to a solitary place, where he prayed" (Mark 1:35). Take your own felt needs and the needs of those you lead before your heavenly Father.
2. Create "safe spaces" to truly hear from men. This will take time. These safe spaces will depend on the needs and likes of your men. Some guys will open up over coffee or breakfast. For others, you may want to organize a group outing, such as bowling, hunting, paintballing, or a sporting event. Travel together and weave in time for conversation.
3. Make your men feel comfortable, appreciated, and cared for. When that happens, they will share how life is going for them.

EVALUATE AND DISCERN

When a country is rebellious, it has many rulers, but a ruler with discernment and knowledge maintains order. (Proverbs 28:2)

Having a discerning spirit as you listen and lead requires the ability to be both surrendered to God's purposes and responding to the needs of those around you. Responding to the needs of your men doesn't mean you give up your authority. Just the opposite! Authority comes from meeting the needs of a group and reflecting both truth and grace.

1. Leading men well will require that you recruit other men and leaders who share similar beliefs and thoughts on what it means to be a godly leader and man. If not, conflicting messages from

those in leadership will ultimately communicate chaos and ineffectiveness.

2. Surround yourself with an inner circle of men who speak truth and grace into your own life. Some great questions to ask these men are, "How am I truly doing? Where are some of my blind spots in my leadership?"

3. Don't minister in a vacuum. Track what other churches, groups, and ministries are doing. This is not to compare or compete, but to gain fresh ideas and strategies.

NO STRINGS ATTACHED

I have become all things to all people so that by all possible means I might save some. I do all this for the sake of the gospel, that I may share in its blessings. (1 Corinthians 9:22–23)

The purpose of leading and listening is ultimately for the benefit of the people God puts in our charge, as well as to give glory, not to ourselves, but to the one we serve. In my speaking and travels, I have heard from many men who are tired of "angles." Everyone is "selling" something. Men long for relationships that don't have strings attached. This includes the gospel.

Obviously, we want all men to know the hope of the gospel. We need to lead, build relationships, and speak truth well. But we can't play the Holy Spirit in the lives of men. We need to love them right where they are, creating spaces for authenticity and vulnerability, as we open the Word of God together. Isn't that the entire point of men's fellowship and ministry? Commit to listening to each other in such a way that opens the door for Christ to transform you and the men you lead from the inside out.

There's great motivation in the image described in 2 Chronicles 16:9: "For the eyes of the LORD range throughout the earth to strengthen those whose hearts are fully committed to him." If you long to partner with God, then lead with love and strengthen hearts. Begin by opening your own heart to the hearts of your men. Quite simply, LISTEN.

13

HOW TO HELP A MAN DISCOVER HIS CALLING

(GARY BARKALOW)

Gary Barkalow has been studying and speaking about calling for more than twenty-five years. He is the author of *It's Your Call* and founder of The Noble Heart Ministry, helping you discover the life you were created to live that brings life to others. Contact Gary at gary@TheNobleHeart.com or visit TheNobleHeart.com.

> *Calling is the most comprehensive reorientation and the most profound motivation in human experience.*
> —Os Guinness

Shortly after a man encounters Jesus, he may begin to wonder about his calling: *Who am I really? What purpose has God given me?* This question of a God-given calling cannot be answered in a single moment of time or in isolation. It is a progressive revelation, with more to be revealed only after we walk into what has already been revealed. It also requires the eyes of brothers. We are too close to our own life for clarity. As you walk with a man in his journey with God, you can play a critical role in the discovery, development, and deployment of his calling.

The medical profession determines a trauma victim's degree of consciousness by the patient's ability to state his name, date, and location. If he can, he is considered "alert and oriented times three"

(A&Ox3)—fully aware and responsive. To help a man discover his calling, we must help him live alert and oriented to his God-given desires, story, and journey.

To help a man be A&Ox3, you must have a *heartcentric* approach: heart-based, not skills-based. Most men have experienced affirmation solely for the tasks they can accomplish. But task fulfillment does not express who they truly are.

Competence identity is purely a worldly, utilitarian philosophy. It proclaims that we are what we do rather than the biblical proclamation of a God-given weightiness in who we are. This ungodly perspective has distorted our understanding of calling and encouraged us to define calling in terms of a mere title, job description, or place (pastor, missionary, plumber, or accountant). The result of this thinking is either debilitating discouragement or an exhausting, insincere life of imitation.

ALERT AND ORIENTED TO DESIRE

Jesus said, "Each tree is recognized by its own fruit. ... A good man brings good things out of the good stored up in his heart" (Luke 6:44–45). The distinct, God-designed fruitfulness of a man's life is an expression of his calling; it is recognizable by the God-given desires of his redeemed heart. Paul said it this way, "By [God's] power he may bring to fruition your every desire for goodness and your every deed prompted by faith" (2 Thessalonians 1:11).

Our calling is to offer our unique "desire for goodness" to the world. It is the brilliance and compelling of his life as revealed in his God-created desires. Scripture says, "For it is God who is producing in you both the desire and the *ability* to do what pleases him" (Philippians 2:13 ISV). The good news is that what we are *supposed* to do is what we most *want* to do. Therefore, we need to help a man explore his heart by giving permission and pathways to his God-given desires.

Men tend to "be all or nothing" when it comes to desire. They either live a life of selfish ambition (see Philippians 2:3–4) or heartless obedience (see Matthew 15:8). "Desire" is an arena that must be explored with a discerning heart and discerning friends. The Bible says, "He who separates himself seeks his own desire, he quarrels against all sound wisdom" (Proverbs 18:1 NASB), and "Examine everything carefully; hold fast to that which is good" (1 Thessalonians 5:21 NASB).

The heart will reveal itself through questions. Here are some questions that may reveal a man's "desire for goodness":

- What movies have you loved? Why? What character? Why? What scene? Why?
- What books or speakers have you loved? Why? What point captured you the most?
- If you could go to school to study anything, what would it be?
- Describe a compliment that you were given that moved you to tears?
- Describe a time when you felt most alive, in your sweet spot, doing something with an acute awareness of the life of God within you?
- What is it that moves you from "someone has to do something about this" to "I have to do something about this"?

Be aware that what is revealed about a man's heart and desires through these questions is probably not the truest, most accurate picture of his calling. Like looking at a picture in a travel brochure, there is much more to your destination than you are currently seeing.

ALERT AND ORIENTED TO STORY

To help a man discover his calling, we must be *storycentric* as well as heartcentric. Information is helpful in a context. Our life story is that context. Experiences, examined by themselves, can be misleading; they must be looked at in the framework of a man's life.

Most men have never really told their story—unscripted, uninterrupted, and unedited. A man may have shared his testimony or shared a traumatic moment, but that was more like a movie clip, not his entire story. I have been enthralled by a movie trailer only to be surprised, after seeing the movie, that I misunderstood what the short clip was all about. I assumed that I understood the story from the three-minute trailer. It's easy to do this with another man's life.

Something profound takes place when a man tells his complete story. It is even more powerful when he shares his story with a few men, who in turn tell their stories. Hearing another man's story often clarifies a bit of our own story that we never understood before. To understand a man's story, I have found some helpful strategies.

First, have him think through his life before he tells his story, writing down key moments, settings, and relationships. Here are some categories to stimulate memory:

- List each place you've lived and describe what life was like for you there.
- List each school you went to and describe what life was like during those years.
- List the people who were a part of your life and describe what impact they had on you.
- List the social circles you were in (academics, church, sports, music, technology, party, fraternity, work, military) and describe what effect they had on you.
- List your work experiences and describe what life was like for you there.

Second, establish ground rules:

- Maintain confidentiality.
- Do not interpret, edit, or counsel a man while he tells his story.
- You may only ask clarifying questions, such as: How old are you at this point? Where are your parents at this point? What happened in that five-year gap in your story?

Third, as you listen, look for answers to these questions:

- What did he love?
- What did he dislike?
- How was he wounded and/or hurt? And what did he consequently believe about himself, the world, relationships, and God?

- What did he do well?
- What did he not do well?
- How did God choreograph circumstances and people in his life?
- Who were the major influences in his life? What did they deposit?
- Observe his countenance (often the heart will reveal what the mouth cannot speak):
  - When his eyes are big and bright or cast down and dull, what is he talking about?
  - When his mannerisms are animated or low-key, what is he talking about?
  - When his voice is clear and bold or quiet and distant, what is he talking about?

ALERT AND ORIENTED TO JOURNEY

As God reveals the desires of a man's heart, he also develops the strength of his heart so that he can handle his desires well. Too many men have mishandled their desires, even good desires, because they lacked the wisdom and character to wield them well in this fallen world. The expression of their calling became corrupted, and they moved from acts of faith to acts of flesh. This is the mark of an untrained heart. Godly character takes time to develop.

This much-needed strength of heart is not acquired simply through experience, but only through *evaluated* experience. Just because we've gone through something doesn't mean that we've *grown* from it. If we want to find gold, we need to learn to dig. Self-evaluation is like cutting your own hair. We can see some strands but other strands are hidden from us. It is possible to evaluate one's experiences alone, but it is more effective when it is done with another.

When helping a man evaluate an experience, I suggest questions like these:

- How were your actions received?
- Was your serving/offering accepted or rejected? Why?
- Did you bring them life?

- Did your actions or words change anything in terms of direction, attitude, perspective, or outcomes? Why?
- What would you do differently next time? Why?
- How did you experience it?
- What was going on in your heart as you offered it? What was the condition of your heart: scared, stressed, angry, at peace, confident, confused? Why? What do you think that was about?
- Has this given you more clarity about your calling?
- Even if it was unsuccessful, did having this experience bring you life?
- What were the motives of your heart?
- What were you hoping for?
- How did your heart react to the reaction of others?
- Did you feel connected to or disconnected with God in the process?
- What do you believe that God is saying to you through this?
- How do you think that God is training you in this?

Remember, a man's answer is just the beginning of the truth. Go deeper. Follow your curiosity. He will allow you to do this if he trusts your motivation.

To help a man discover his calling, help him become alert and oriented to his desires, story, and journey. He will need heart-, story-, and journeycentric questions and connections.

Section IV

MEN AND SMALL GROUPS

14

SMALL GROUPS: THE LIFEBLOOD OF MINISTRIES FOR MEN

(DAVID MEEKINS)

David Meekins is the Celebrate Recovery pastor at The Bridge Church of Santa Rosa and a speaker, trainer, and coach with The John Maxwell Leadership Team. His daily goal is to give a message of hope to everyone he meets, that personal growth and life change can happen through the transforming power of Jesus Christ. Contact David at dmeekins@comcast.net.

For many men, small groups are the foundation of their spiritual lives. Small groups often capture the heart of a man at his point of need. The group gives him a sense of belonging and gets him out of isolation and loneliness.

Men's groups are also a strategic entry point for men into your church and community. For new recruits, they offer a casual, nonthreatening, safe place to be heard and accepted. Affinity groups centered around softball, shooting sports, bicycle riding, motorcycles, fishing, and other activities are safe for the nonchurched man. Men may feel like they have to be a Bible expert or have their act together before they go to church, but a small affinity group can be much more welcoming.

WHAT MODEL SHOULD WE USE?

Simply put, use the model that works best for your men and your target audience. Don't try to replicate a Southern California or Florida model if you live in Alaska or Kansas. It won't work and will leave you and your men frustrated.

You can implement a *quarterly rally* with your weekly small groups. The large rally or community service project builds a sense of purpose and community. While small groups create an opportunity for personal relationships, a large-group setting lets them know they are a part of an entire community of men.

You can also have *weekly men's large-group* meetings at church for worship, short teaching, or videos. When the teaching is over, break your men into small groups with a consistent table leader for more intimate connecting. Small-group leaders direct follow-up discussion, facilitate prayer requests, invite confidential sharing, and establish accountability.

Small groups can meet at any time and in any place. The men's pastor can coordinate schedules, recommend resources, and offer training for leaders. In this model, your leaders carry much of the responsibility for keeping their group on task and moving forward.

HOW DO I FIND LEADERS?

Make a list of the men you think might be available to step up and lead. And then pray over it. Pray God clearly identifies and calls the right men your way. Seek men who are faithful and committed, specifically to the needs of other men. Look also for fruit in their lives. Observe their marriages (if married) and how they conduct themselves with members of the opposite sex. Take your time. You want a few good, qualified men.

One strategy is to ask men for help. I try to never do a task alone. Something as routine as making coffee and setting up chairs is an opportunity to find men who have a heart for service. These are times to ask questions and listen. Men rise to the level of our expectations. I have found some of my best leaders this way. Also, ask your *initial* team of leaders who they believe might be potential recruits.

CARING FOR YOUR LEADERS

Leading a small group can be difficult. Expect occasional bouts of discouragement, weariness, and even doubt. Plan times for your leaders to relax and recharge. A new or renewed vision can go a long way in rekindling energy and passion.

Make sure each small group has an assistant or coleader, taking some responsibility and pressure off the primary group leader. A coleader can take over when the primary leader is sick, traveling, or just needs a break.

Schedule time off for your leaders. They need time away to recharge, even if it's just a week or a month. A sabbatical will help them stay committed for the long haul.

Sharpen your leaders with resources, such as books, CDs, or links to well-done podcasts and webinars. Take your leaders to a men's conference and pay for it. A tangible gift goes a long way to say, "I appreciate you." You are building into their lives as they build into the lives of others.

ANONYMITY AND CONFIDENTIALITY

A man's trust is hard to gain and easy to lose. Most men will not share their deep secrets and struggles if they do not feel their group will keep confidences.

"Larry" shared about his wife's battle with depression and how it was really affecting him. A few weeks later, when Larry and his wife were together with other couples, a member of his men's group asked Larry's wife how she was doing with her depression. Whoops! Larry will probably never share again—and I can't really blame him.

If you are in a one-on-one conversation with a man on a sensitive issue, move to the side of the group to protect confidentiality and avoid eavesdroppers.

HOW TO KEEP YOUR GROUP FRESH

Routines can become ruts. A rut is a grave with the ends knocked out. We don't want our groups to die. How can we avoid this? Here are a number of things to implement:

Invite one of your men to share a testimony. You might find some great communicators in your ranks.

Bring in a guest speaker. One night I had my young-adult daughters come and share. I told my girls to share freely, the good, the bad, and the ugly about me as their father. I must say they had a little fun at my expense! The men could ask any question they wanted. It was a memorable night for the men, my daughters, and me.

Skip the lesson one night and do something fun. Our ministry to men is more important than the ministry machine—getting through the lessons. Go bowling, miniature golfing, or shoot pool. These activities appeal to the men on the fringes who hear about all the fun we are having.

Mix up your studies. Do a topical Bible study, then a chapter book, followed by a serious expository study. Sometimes have the group vote on what to do next.

Keep things light. When opening Scripture, I often say, "Men, take your Bibles and turn to the very front. There is a table of contents, just like any other book. Don't be afraid to use it." I always wait until I see that all the men have found the passage before I begin the lesson. It's rewarding to see men asking for help from other men. That means your group is comfortable together. Starting when a man is still flipping pages is demeaning. If they are asking, "Can you help me grow as a man of God?" and we are not patient as they stumble along at first, we will lose them.

HANDLING DIFFICULT PEOPLE

Every small group has difficult people. Some want to dominate the group discussion, while others follow rabbit trails. Some love to stir up discord surrounding political and theological issues. Still others love to gossip. What do you do?

At your first meeting, agree to a set of guidelines and read them periodically (at the beginning of each month, for example, or more frequently if needed). Emphasize that as the group facilitator, you will ensure these guidelines are followed—for everyone's benefit. When individuals get off track, and they will, remind them with a spirit of gentleness that you need to adhere to the guidelines. Oftentimes, other members of the group will ask the offender to abide by the rules. That way you don't have to be the "bad guy" every time.

Pray for the Holy Spirit's guidance. You might be ready to cut a man off at the very moment he's ready to reveal a personal struggle. Avoid setting a tone that silences the group. And pray for wisdom and ask for feedback on how you are doing. Believe me, your group will let you know. As the book of Proverbs says, "The wise man seeks counsel" (12:15).

PRAYER AND PRAYER REQUESTS

Prayer may be one of the most valuable tools in building a cohesive, caring group. Once a month or between studies, you may want to spend your entire time sharing prayer requests and answered prayers. Or take a set amount of time at the end of every meeting to share pressing needs. Remind your group that the same rules apply to your prayer times. No gossip. No dominating the floor. Give everyone a chance to participate.

Prayer communicates that individuals matter. It admits our dependence on God. Praying out loud models how to pray for newer Christians. It allows men in your group to minister to each other, something that rarely happens outside of a small group environment. And it focuses on the Creator, who cares for every man in your group.

Finally, if you're a men's pastor, make sure you get in a vibrant, challenging, audacious small group yourself, especially one where you are *not* the leader or coleader.

15

HOW TO SET UP REAL AND PRACTICAL ACCOUNTABILITY

(ROD HANDLEY)

Rod Handley is founder and president of Character that Counts (CTC), which is based in Kansas City, Missouri. Rod has written over twenty books and speaks extensively to men, women, and teens about "character, integrity, and accountability" issues. As former COO/CFO for Fellowship of Christian Athletes, he continues to work with a number of NFL, NBA, and MLB teams. Contact Rod at rhandley@kc.rr .com or visit characterthatcounts.org.

Accountability. Men are afraid of the word. By definition, it means to "report, explain, or justify yourself to another person." Who really wants to do this? My human nature wants to run from accountability. Yet, in my pursuit of character (doing right) and integrity (being whole), accountability is crucial to me becoming the person God wants me to be.

Temptations are real and they are powerful. Our flesh, sin nature, and satan himself constantly challenges our faith. Many ministry leaders have suffered visible public failures, destroying their ministries and families as secret sin was exposed. Everyone can fall. Every Christian needs accountability in his or her life. If you are not a part of an accountability group, I urge you to join one. Your church may already offer these groups. If not, then consider starting one of your own or launching a program on behalf of your entire church body.

Starting an accountability group is easier than one might think. Do you know a Christian man who is serious about living a faithful life? Ask him to meet with you weekly. Pray for three or four others to join you. Over time, God will help identify potential candidates for your group. You're looking for:

- Men who love the Lord and whose relationship with Christ is a high priority. If the man is not a believer, accountability is not a good option for him. If you want to pursue a non-Christian relationship, this is an evangelistic opportunity. Accountability is designed to be done with someone headed in the same direction as you.

- Men who want to see you succeed. They will be an encouragement and a cheerleader, as well as be willing to confront you honestly and directly. There must be shared respect and trust in each other's judgment.

- Men who can stretch you, as well as those who will be challenged by you. A current friend or coworker may or may not be a candidate due to the history you already share together. Another obvious possibility may be a family member. You will need to pray about this one.

- Men of all ages, races, cultures, and marital statuses. Accountability works well when the people in the group are different than you. There is only one prohibition: accountability should not be done with a person of the opposite sex.

Remember, this is not a "sin management" group. Your group mind-set should be "totally understandable, totally unacceptable." You are not getting together to manage sin, but to eradicate it.

I encourage groups to meet weekly. During a week, numerous opportunities emerge that need to be communicated or addressed. If you meet less frequently, it will become far too casual as details and specifics grow fuzzy. Furthermore, if one or two members can't meet, the others can still gather even if it is just two members. With modern technology, Skype is also an option for people to connect from any location.

Groups can meet in homes, churches, coffee shops, or restaurants. In the early years, our group met at a local Denny's in one of the back-corner tables. Many establishments welcome regular groups in private rooms and secluded alcoves. The key is finding an area where you can talk openly and confidentially.

Every accountability time begins and ends with prayer. Occasionally, you may want to include a planned devotional or Bible study. Often, the ending prayer will be an extended time where everyone participates, bringing various requests before the Lord.

From time to time, our group welcomes out-of-town visitors who want to see how accountability works, and the men observing have always been amazed with the candid and genuine conversation.

Our group has a long history of doing life outside of our meetings, including weekend camping trips with spouses and kids, golfing, attending Kansas City Royals and Chiefs games, cookouts, service projects, mission trips, and so on. These times deepen the friendship we share and make our weekly time together even more special.

Different than a typical small group, recruiting for accountability groups is a little more controlled. An intentional individual invitation increases the chances a man will make a long-term commitment to the group. You may have a wide age range, but there's still likely to be an affinity or unifying characteristic to any long-term accountability circle.

It's worth noting that small groups of mature high school boys can also hold one another accountable. My sons began meeting with the teen sons of two of my accountability partners during their high school years, and the experience helped them grow in their faith, friendship, and responsibility as Christian men.

There are some men who will go AWOL. In fact, prepare for this to occur, because accountability reveals and exposes truth and the sin which so easily entangles all of us. Challenge those men in a loving way to keep coming weekly. Don't stop asking the hard questions, but make it a point to celebrate victories. Ultimately, they must decide if they really want the group to hold them to the covenants. If they want to be released, strongly encourage them to pursue accountability with a different group of men.

Obviously, there is some risk involved in accountability. A huge question for every man will be, *Can I trust these men with my stuff?* For years, I have told my brothers, "This is not about perfection; it is about direction." Accountability is for imperfect people journeying together, working toward a shared goal by sharpening one another.

To help you get started with your accountability group, consider using the following ten questions my men's group has been using since 1990. These questions are the basis for my book *Character Counts: Who's Counting Yours?*, which answers the *whys* and *hows* of accountability:

1. Have you spent daily time in the Scriptures and in prayer?
2. Have you had any flirtatious or lustful attitudes, tempting thoughts, or exposed yourself to any explicit materials that would not glorify God?
3. Have you been completely above reproach in your financial dealings?
4. Have you spent quality relationship time with family and friends?
5. Have you done your 100 percent best in your job, school, etc.?
6. Have you told any half-truths or outright lies, putting yourself in a better light to those around you?
7. Have you shared the gospel with an unbeliever this week?
8. Have you taken care of your body through daily physical exercise and proper eating and sleeping habits?
9. Have you allowed any person or circumstance to rob you of your joy?
10. Have you lied to us on any of your answers today?

Questions like these are essential for every accountability group. Without them, an accountability group will soon deteriorate to a superficial "news, sports, and weather" conversation. If someone isn't willing to answer with honesty and vulnerability, then they are probably not going to last long in your group.

Equally as important is absolute confidentiality with any of the issues raised during your accountability time. Disclosures are not to be shared with anyone, including spouses, unless approved by the one who is sharing.

Successful accountability groups make a formal covenant with one another. A covenant means "to agree, to be of one mind, to come together." It is a binding and solemn agreement to do or keep from doing something. A covenant solidifies your accountability. A well-established covenant is a gift from God, nurtured by authentic love and sustained by an unwavering commitment.

While the word *accountability* doesn't appear in Scripture, the Bible delivers more than one hundred verses that validate accountable relationships, including "As iron sharpens iron, so one man sharpens another" (Proverbs 27:17) and "Two are better than one, because they have a good return for their labor. If either of them falls down, one can help the other up. But pity anyone who falls and has no one to help them up" (Ecclesiastes 4:9–10). You may even want to do your own Bible study, being sure not to miss Proverbs 9:8–9, 11:14, 12:1, 27:6, Hebrews 3:13, and James 5:16, among others.

Stu Weber once said, "Accountability grows over time. As your relationship and confidence in one another develops, and as your acceptance and affirmation take root, you earn the right to ask the hard questions." It's almost guaranteed. As your trust and vulnerability with your accountability brothers strengthens, your relationship with Christ will also deepen. This, in turn, adds to the love and respect you have for those men in your circle. And this, in turn, invites Christ to be at the center in all your relationships. All of this is designed by the Creator.

16

INITIATING MEN
INTO MANHOOD

(BRIAN CHILDRES)

Brian Childres is the creator of Men's Bootcamp, a weekend God-encounter that has been a catalyst for the East Texas men's revival. He has two awesome children and enjoys bass fishing. Contact Brian at brian@brotherhoodproject.org or visit freedomtrainings.org.

I will never forget the day three of my buddies and I paid a visit to the Ponderosa Ranch in beautiful East Texas. We were eighteen-year-olds full of confidence as we strolled into the welcome center. We were greeted by a seventy-year-old man wearing nothing but tube socks and sandals! He enthusiastically told us about the upcoming volleyball tournament and asked us if we enjoyed horseback riding.

At this point, all we could think about was escaping out the same black gate that we entered through. We thanked the naked man for his time. He told us to be sure to come out the following month for the crowning of Miss Ponderosa. In no time, we were out of there. And we laughed all the way home! That was my first and last visit to the Ponderosa Ranch—Texas' only public nudist resort.

Genesis 3 tells of the first nudist resort ever built. Mankind got off to a perfect start living in Eden Ranch, a community full of naked people. Or, at least two naked people: Adam and Eve. This was God's purpose for every man: to live naked and unashamed. In essence, to enjoy rich relational intimacy, both with God and with others.

The problem is that we too often fall back into the same trap that snared Adam. When God came looking for him, Adam responded, "I heard you in the garden, and I was afraid because I was naked; so I hid" (Genesis 3:10). The first problem of humankind is still the main problem: We hide. And we get into all kinds of trouble when we do so: porn, selfishness, bitterness, greed, and every other maladies of men. It all stems from hiding, also known as isolation.

I am convinced this is man's biggest problem. That's why we began an aggressive campaign to destroy isolation back in 2008. We realized that once a man is set free from isolation, he can begin to truly grow in Christ. Give a man genuine brotherhood and everything changes.

A man's spiritual health depends on having men intimately involved in his spiritual life. Now, we are *not* talking about attending a weekly men's small group, Bible study, or accountability group. Unfortunately, those can function as fig leaves also. Rather, I am talking about vulnerable, intimate, Christ-focused friendships.

Many churches may have an impressive network of men's groups, but fail when it comes to creating true brotherhood. That's why men constantly ask, "How do you build a genuine brotherhood?" Discipling men requires you to first connect men in life-giving relationships, which will only happen when you learn the fine art of initiation.

Initiation is the key to building a masculine army in your church; it is a lost art in our modern society. Yet it is still alive in many corners of the world. For example, boys from the Satere-Mawe tribe in the Amazon must stick a bare hand into a glove swarming with bullet ants. The boys must withstand their stings for ten minutes without making a noise. According to the Schmidt Sting Index, the bullet ant has the worst sting of the ant world. The swelling continues for twenty-four hours and is described as "waves of throbbing, all-consuming pain."

Thankfully, we employ a different method when we initiate men.

We begin by stripping men of everything that keeps them in isolation. Remember Genesis 3? If a man's biggest problem is hiding, then the solution is to lead him out of hiding. All things must come out of the dark and be brought into the light of Christ. In some ways, this can be more painful than the sting of a bullet ant, but it opens the door to the freedom we crave.

The first step of initiation is *confession*. James 5:16 says, "Confess your sins to each other and pray for each other so that you may be healed." This is a profound promise that can bring great freedom to a man who has real brothers. Every man has at least one deep, dark secret. It is impossible to live in freedom when we hide things in the closet of our souls.

The next step is *disclosing our fears*. This is crucial because our fears expose our unbelief, which is our greatest obstacle as men. God simply wants us to trust him. Oftentimes we are blind to the sin of unbelief. Men need to experience the freedom and courage it takes to expose these blind spots.

The third step is *taking off our masks*. Recall those three tragic words from Genesis 3:10: "So I hid." We all hide. We all wear masks. Every man plays the poser who says, "I'm Fine." But before we can take off our masks, we must be able to identify them. Can you relate to any of these masks?

- Mr. Spiritual
- The Answer Man
- The Funny Guy
- Mr. Tough Guy
- The Victim

Hiding our real faces is killing us, as well as hurting those we love. Let's help each other take off the mask so we can breathe again.

The fourth step is *exposing our wounds*. Every man has been hurt; some men have been tragically wounded. Many men live in daily torment because of a single past event. When you give a man a safe place to reveal the gory pain of an open wound, you empower him to take a huge step toward healing.

The fifth and final step is *repenting of idols*. Our idols are oftentimes more destructive than our sins. Why? Because our idols come from the good things in our lives: our marriage, ministry, work, or hobbies. True freedom comes when we recognize our counterfeit gods and turn back to Jesus.

These five steps are crucial if we are serious about building an army of men who are living their lives naked and unashamed.

Every man desires to be initiated. They hunger to be deeply known by others. Men are tired of wearing the mask. Their deep hearts want to come out of hiding, but pride and fear keep them in the chains of isolation. And there they will remain unless we help them get free.

We have created a three-day weekend initiation process called Men's Bootcamp that does this very thing. We don't spend any time teaching, singing, or tossing horseshoes. It is 100 percent initiation. The weekend is a unique spiritual journey designed to help men uncover two simple realities: their desperate need for God and for one another. But be forewarned. This process is not fun. Overcoming pride can be a fierce battle. But it is worth the struggle. Just ask Tom. Here is his experience in his own words:

> I had been in bondage to pornography for twenty-five years. My wife and daughter both had experienced much pain as a result. Three different pastors had let me down in their attempts to help. Finally, I showed up at Men's Bootcamp and found brothers who loved me in the midst of all of my sin. They helped me get to the root of my worthlessness. There was no judgement and a ton of affirmation. I am free today because of the love of these men.

Every man who goes through the journey of initiation receives two priceless gifts: spiritual freedom and genuine brothers. This changes everything for a man. Just remember that initiation is exactly what the name implies—it is simply a beginning. A beginning to a brand-new way of living the Christian life.

Once you are officially a brother, you get all the privileges of membership. Our men come together at a minimum of once a week to SPAR together. Our version of sparring is just as fierce as two fighters in the octagon, except that the intensity is spiritual in nature. SPAR is our acronym for Sharpening, Prayer, Affirmation, and Repentance.

Sharpening is the healthy pain that is experienced in the brotherhood. We help each other get to the heart of the matter by asking probing questions. We also are fearless in giving feedback, helping men to see their blind spots.

Prayer is crucial to the process too. We honestly pour out our hearts to God, surrender our wives and kids, and believe God to move mountains. Above all, we sit silently and listen as God speaks his powerful truth.

Affirmation is simply reminding each other that we have what it takes to live fully as men of God. We passionately declare to each other who we are in Christ. Affirmation is a powerful tool in destroying the enemy's lies.

When men spar, they always experience transformation, a change of heart. Whether it is *repenting* of resentment toward a wife or letting go of financial fear, men always leave a SPAR meeting truly transformed.

The way God is moving in the men of East Texas is nothing new. We are simply joining the revolution that began with Jesus and twelve weak men two thousand years ago. Whether you join us onsite or use these principles to launch your own brotherhood, we challenge all men to be real with one another and watch God do miracles, one man at a time. Will you join the revolution?

Section V

MINISTERING
TO SUBGROUPS
OF MEN

17

PASS THE BATON: ENCOURAGING AND EQUIPPING DADS

(RICK WERTZ)

Rick Wertz is the founder and president of Faithful Fathering. After fifteen years in the corporate world, Rick founded Faithful Fathering in 2000 to encourage and equip dads to be faithful fathers and raise the next godly generation. Go to faithfulfathering.org or e-mail admin@faithfulfathering.org.

There were men from churches all over our community at the luncheon. Each church had its own table. In the middle of our table was a sharp-looking binder, silver in color with a logo that read "Faithful Fathering" and a one-liner, "Dads Becoming Heroes." There was also a silver baton—like the ones used in a track relay race—beside the binder.

Over lunch, the founder of Faithful Fathering gave a testimony of his journey as a dad. He spoke of how he had been blessed with a happy and healthy marriage and family, something he had not known in the home he grew up in. But he had allowed himself to get busy chasing success in a job involving long hours and a lot of traveling.

Our speaker had grown up below the poverty line and was determined to provide for his family. One Saturday morning, he returned home from another extended business trip. He kissed his wife and headed straight back to the office to wrap up paperwork and plan for meetings Monday morning. He glanced out the back window and asked his bride, "Who is that out there playing with our daughter?"

"That's our son," she replied. "You're traveling too much."

At that moment, the Holy Spirit delivered a message that was clear, accurate, and convicting: "Son, I have answered your prayers and you are taking these blessings for granted. And I am losing a generation because of dads like you."

The room went completely silent.

Then the speaker issued a simple challenge to every father present: Pass the baton. He challenged every church to train its men in this important work. PASS is an acronym that refers to Purpose-filled father, Accelerate learning to be a dad, Stay connected, and Start the movement.

PASS THE BATON

Purpose-filled fathering is a call for dads to be intentional. The speaker confessed passivity in his role as a father. Fathers are called to be more than financial providers and disciplinarians. Faithful fathers prioritize physical presence, are engaged emotionally, and lead spiritually by example. As I listened, that call pierced my own heart.

Accelerate learning to be a dad is a charge to take responsibility. As fathers, we typically do what our dad did, or we go in the *opposite* direction. Neither is necessarily right or healthy. I was certainly in that camp. I had a good dad, and I was trying to carry on his legacy by being a good dad for my kids. The speaker asked a question that got my attention: "How does your church resource and train dads for the most important job in the world, being a dad?" My reluctant answer was that we do nothing specifically to encourage or equip dads. I eagerly took note of resources he mentioned that might help me be the dad God called me to be.

Staying connected through the transitions of fathering requires diligence. Fathers pass through three phases: teacher, coach, and counselor. The teacher phase is when Dad and Mom are the primary, almost sole, influence in a child's life. All instruction is taken as absolute, and there is little to no pushback. This may last up to age six or eight, maybe even until ten.

The coach phase is when outside influences of friends, teachers, extended family, or others open the door to new perspectives. Coaching a child well through worldly experiences will provide reinforcement of the earlier teaching and encourage the child to embrace the absolutes taught as his or her own. This phase requires being engaged as kids stumble and even fail in areas of life. Failure is part of life, and a coach uses failures as stepping-stones for growth. In extreme circumstances, the coach can call a time-out and change the environment if it is negative or dangerous. Coaching is a dad's role from eight to eighteen, with it sometimes lasting into the child's early twenties.

The counselor phase is what it implies; the father is available but does not force himself into his children's lives. His young-adult child must ask for counsel. One of the toughest responsibilities of this phase is letting go. Dad should continue to pray, invite his kids to lunch, and let them know the door is always open for emergencies. But trying to teach or coach at this point is not healthy. Men require support as they navigate the teacher-coach-counselor transitions.

Starting the movement means initiating a mission for dads in the church and beyond. Paul writes, "Fathers, do not exasperate your children; instead, bring them up in the training and instruction of the Lord" (Ephesians 6:4). The second half of that verse calls dads out to be on mission in their families. The hearts of fathers must turn from the busyness in the world to right priorities that glorify the Father.

STARTING A MOVEMENT WITHIN YOUR CHURCH

Every church should establish a core group of dads who are willing to build relationships and be accountable to one another. This leads to the BATON strategy.

Begin. Recognize the need to encourage and equip dads specifically in the role as a father:

- Create a buzz around fathering.
- Convey the connection between the Father and fathers.
- Reflect on the triune nature of God: spiritual, physical, and emotional.

- Build on that in your own relationship with your children—leading spiritually, being present physically, and engaging emotionally.
- Commit to spearheading your own fathering movement.

Assimilate like minds. Foster the vision to encourage dads on their journey as a father:

- Create a core group and initiate regular meetings.
- Identify eight to ten male lay leaders with one or two staff who have diverse gifts and demographics that match your church and community.
- Establish regularly scheduled meetings, committing to one or two hours every month.
- Build relationships and schedule a kickoff event.

Transition. Initiate the process to engage dads in raising a godly generation:

- Be contagious as a core group of dads who are accountable to each other.
- Develop a unique mission and vision that complements the church's mission and vision.
- Conduct a kickoff event.
- Bring in compelling speakers with targeted talks, such as "A Father's Legacy is the Sum of His Choices."

Ongoing management. Drive the process to engage dads in raising a godly generation:

- Review and assess your kickoff event and build on the response and momentum.
- Schedule and execute future steps. Think both short and long term.
- Consider two to three fun, easy-to-plug-into events that bring dads and kids together.
- Offer one or two studies for dads. A Sunday school series or a stand-alone study for dads.

- Hold one strategic weekend retreat per year—for dads, fathers and daughters, or fathers and sons.
- Reinforce your core group, offer ongoing enrichment, and rotate in new dads.

N*etwork*. Extend the strategy and broaden your network as contagious Christians in the community:

- Identify and equip a network of "point dads."
- Target tangential groups of dads within the body and community.
- Encourage point dads to take responsibility to represent the core group by connecting with other dads who have kids in a specific age range.
- Coordinate unique activities and events for specific demographics.
- Look for creative ways to engage other groups within the church and community.

The BATON strategy has proven to be a practical approach for us to grow as fathers and to engage other dads in the church. It was over two years ago that a group of us attended that luncheon. Today, our core group is ten lay leaders strong, and there are two staff members on the team. The kickoff event held three months into the process attracted eighty-five dads.

Over the first year, we conducted three easy-to-engage events for dads and kids that encouraged men to be more intentional in their fathering—a fishing outing, a fun day on church grounds, and a canoe trip. There was devotion time incorporated with each event. We also had a summer study specifically for dads called "Dads Becoming Heroes."

During the second year, there were three more easy-to-engage events: a second annual fishing outing, another canoe trip, and a trip to the zoo for dads with young kids. We conducted a second summer study, "A Dad's Armor," and we coordinated a father-daughter adventure weekend that helped a number of dads transition from the teaching to the coaching phase of fathering.

Each of us in the core group has been blessed individually and in family through relationships built on this journey. Dads across the entire church—and unchurched dads in the community—have also been blessed by the fun activities and events. In just two years, we have witnessed an increasingly positive and enthusiastic buzz around fathering in our church. We are committed to pass the baton well to the next generation of dads.

18

COMING ALONGSIDE
SINGLE FATHERS

(MATT HAVILAND)

Matt Haviland is the founder and director of A Father's Walk, a single-dad ministry; he is an author and a speaker. He lives in Grand Rapids, Michigan, with his wife and daughter. For more information, visit afatherswalk.org.

In January of 2008, I was a new convert in Christ with a twenty-month-old daughter. Her mother and I were never married. As the court battles raged on, I was trying to establish at least *some* custody.

One evening, the leader of a men's small group I had recently joined asked a question that rocked me: "What are you working on that is big for the kingdom?" I didn't know how to answer that. I was new to the faith, struggling to keep my own life together, and the only single dad in our group.

Wait a minute! I thought to myself. *I'm the only single dad here!* After a quick online search of topics, such as fatherless children and single fathers, I was on to something important. Three months later, with the guidance of other men's ministry leaders, I launched a ministry for single dads.

Today, there are still only a handful of single dad ministries available nationwide. That needs to change. Whether you are looking to plant a ministry for single fathers in your church, start a group out of your home, or perhaps even mentor a single father one-on-one, here are some things to keep in mind.

WHO HE IS

What do you think of when you hear the term "single father"? *Absentee father. Deadbeat dad. He abandoned his family.*

The truth is that most single dads are responsible men. Some are widowers. Some were abandoned by their wives. A single father can be a man with solo custody of his children, primary or equal custody, noncustodial (less than 50 percent), or even someone who currently has no custody but wants to be involved. He's a family member, neighbor, or coworker.

Society honors and elevates single moms and their heroic struggles. Doesn't it make sense to do to the same for hardworking and virtuous single dads? Everyone benefits when a man invests in his children. When we begin to see single fathers as a valued asset and champion for their children, we catch a glimpse of how life's most difficult circumstances can become the greatest of testimonies.

WHERE HE IS

Single dads are everywhere. In many cases, they're around, even if they are not immediately present in the lives of their children. I know plenty of single fathers who were raised in the church and still attend regularly. For whatever reason, they found themselves in brokenness: a broken marriage, a broken home, and now a broken heart.

Over the years, I have seen men abandon their families. But I have seen moms do the same, leaving a dad to parent the children completely alone. You probably have single dads in your faith community. You see them every day in the mall, the grocery store, or at the gym. They're in the jails, halfway houses, and rehabilitation centers. A high percentage of those men are there because they lacked a strong father figure of their own. If no one steps into the lives of these single dads and teaches them how to raise their children in Christ, the cycle of fatherlessness and dysfunction is bound to keep repeating itself.

WHY HE MATTERS

When fathers are involved in the lives of their children—full- or part-time—those children perform significantly better overall cognitively, emotionally, socially, and academically.[1] Children from fatherless homes account for 71 percent of high school dropouts (boys drop out on a four to one ratio compared to girls), 75 percent of all teens in chemical abuse centers, 85 percent of those in jail or prison, and 90 percent of homeless and runaway teens.[2] If we want to stop the bleeding in this nation when it comes to crime, teen pregnancy, suicide, substance abuse, divorce, and so on, then we *must* reach the dads.

Single fathering is tough. Consider the court hearing that goes the wrong way, leaving a dad shattered in heartbreak. Or when another man moves into his ex-wife's house with her and the children. Or the overbearing weight of financially supporting two homes and still trying to be a good father along the way. Ministry leaders should be equipped to support dads who find themselves in these traumatic circumstances.

HOW TO COME ALONGSIDE HIM

Who should lead a group for single dads? Ideally, a current or former single father who has been "in the trenches," someone who understands what single dads are going through, and is walking with Jesus. If a pastor takes the lead, make sure he carries out the ministry with grace and compassion, rather than judgment. I'm fortunate enough (if you can call it that) to have walked the same difficult path as many other single fathers, and God has used my experience to share his faithfulness through it all.

CONSISTENCY WITH YOUR GROUP

I used to base my success as a leader on the number of men in our group or the external progress we were making (Facebook followers, number of articles I wrote, attendance at events). What I've learned, however, is being consistent in the men's lives and building trust is the most important benchmark. That's how we help rebuild these men to be the fathers they were created to be. Jon is a fellow single father who said, "If this group wasn't in my life, I wouldn't have a place to go." It's statements like these that keep me going.

THE GOLDEN RULE (FOR YOUR MINISTRY)

One of the top rules we observe in our group is never slam the moms. Yes, we may vent … a lot. But when that turns to slander or trash talking, we put the hammer down. Let your dads talk it out, but encourage them to keep their hearts soft. For better or worse, the way we speak of our children's mother sets the tone for how our sons view women and how our daughters feel about themselves. Teach the dads to use words that build up (see Ephesians 4:29), emphasizing their biblical responsibility to show their children how to honor their mother (see Ephesians 6:4; Exodus 20:12).

I once heard a pastor say, "Our choices today will affect a minimum of three generations: ours, our children's, and our grandchildren's." I would say this statement applies to us as leaders too. This year, 40.3 percent of children born in the United States to women between the ages of 15 and 44 will be born out of wedlock.[3] Our choice to minister, or not minister, to single parents can have the same generational impact. It is up to us as leaders to determine if we will allow fatherlessness to continue or begin to heal single-parent families through Christ.

Being a part of a ministry to single dads has helped me build a phenomenal relationship with my daughter. I would pray that your church would join us in ministering to single dads so we can begin to transform generations to come, one family at a time.

19

HELPING DADS DECODE THEIR DAUGHTERS

(DR. MICHELLE WATSON)

Dr. Michelle Watson is a counselor, host of the radio show *The Dad Whisperer*, and author of the book *Dad, Here's What I Really Need from You: A Guide for Connecting with Your Daughter's Heart.* Contact her at drmichelle@thedad whisperer.com.

"I have no idea what to do," Dave hesitantly admitted as he sat across from me in my counseling office. His relationship with his daughter was broken, and he was desperate for answers. She was having suicidal thoughts, and neither he nor his wife knew how to help her.

"I don't know how my daughter got here," he said. "She has so much going for her. And yes, we've known that starting high school has been challenging for her, but how could she want to end her life? I've tried to be supportive, but now she hardly talks to me. She seems to only open up to her mother, and I don't know how to reach her."

Dave continued, "My wife is a Christian with strong faith and has been trying to live a life that honors God, and she certainly hopes all our children will follow Jesus. I'm also a Christian but with little faith; therefore, I could hardly become the head of the house, leading my whole family in pursuit of God."

Dave's story is all too common. When it comes to their daughters, many fathers are stepping back rather than stepping up. Men are often keenly aware of their weaknesses and will often give up rather than be found incompetent. Add in the complexity of fathering a daughter whose needs intensify as she matures, and even many good fathers are losing the battle for their daughters' hearts.

Helping dads decode their daughters is a passion for me. I've mentored teenage and twentysomething girls for over thirty-five years and been a professional counselor for two decades. In that time, I've had the privilege of helping thousands of dads better relate to their daughters. A few years ago, I founded a ministry to fathers of daughters, and I've authored a book that equips dads to connect with their daughters' hearts. It's hard work, but I keep at it because of the amazing victories I see every day.

Perhaps you work with men like Dave who are estranged from their daughters. Maybe you're in the midst of this storm yourself. Here's the first thing I tell these dads: Despite all the evidence to the contrary, your daughters need you. There is always hope.

Since I live on Venus and you, Dad, live on Mars, I want you to hear something I don't think you hear enough: Not only are you important, but *you are vital to your daughter's health and well-being*—even if her words and behavior at times speak to the contrary. I also want you to know that you matter ... a lot. Without your active engagement, your daughter will suffer.

Though I don't claim to have a corner on all things female, when it comes to coaching dads of daughters, I do know some insider secrets regarding what girls need from their dads in order to thrive. Here are six things every dad needs to know.

SHE LONGS FOR YOUR APPROVAL

If your daughter has given you the message that you are unnecessary, don't believe it. She is desperate for your approval and affirmation, and if she doesn't get what she needs from you, she'll go looking for it elsewhere. She will internalize your view of her, which is why it's imperative to positively, consistently, and intentionally invest in her—with words, time, and attention.

EVEN IF SHE PUSHES YOU AWAY, DON'T LEAVE

It often saddens me to hear dads assume they aren't valuable in the lives of their daughters, particularly as they head into puberty. This is when many men back off and say to Mom, "You're a female, so you deal with her." I understand this is when girls are less predictable, more verbal, and way more emotional, making it very challenging for dads. But it's important to know that this is when hormones begin to rage in her body and brain (over which she has no control since it's about estrogen surging through her body), and they impact her moods, behavior, and thinking.

The reality is that she needs you *even more* during these years, Dad. If you back away, your daughter might assume she's not worth loving and may conclude that something is wrong with her due to your distance or absence. Your presence (aka, moving toward her and initiating time together) lets her know she is valuable and loved.

SHE NEEDS YOU TO RESPOND GENTLY

Just know that it goes a long way to keeping her heart open when you speak kindly, gently, tenderly, and patiently to her. Then if you want to hit it out of the ballpark, add these seven words, "I want to understand. Help me understand." These words align with Malachi 4:6, where God directs fathers to *turn their hearts*—not just their heads—toward their kids. Heart turns may not come as natural for men, but if a dad is open, his daughter can teach him what she needs so he can pace with her.

LIGHT UP WHEN YOU SEE HER

Your daughter is innately wired with the need to be the sparkle (or light) in someone's eyes. And because you were the first man who saw and embraced her, she will turn less to the counterfeit if she has experienced the real thing with you. When you consistently make relational deposits that pour joy into your daughter's heart and life, she will *become* that sparkle, that source of joy to you and others.

MAKE SURE TO DROP THE ANGER

When dads of daughters ask me for my number one piece of advice, I *always* say, "Make sure to drop your anger." Then I add: "Anger is the number one way to hurt your daughter's heart. So make a commitment right here, right now not to respond in anger as a way to assert your power, because it is the most effective way to destroy her and close up her spirit."

We know that "a gentle answer deflects anger" (Proverbs 15:1), yet dad after dad has told me that he either doesn't like the soft approach or says there is no way he can pull back his anger when his daughter's emotions escalate. But a dad *must take the lead* in deescalating himself emotionally or else healing the relationship with his daughter won't happen. Take a "time-out" before responding (I suggest taking an equivalent number of minutes as your age) so you don't say something you'll regret. Then your response will truly match your heart.

SHE WANTS YOU TO ENGAGE
WITH HER SPIRITUALLY

You might be pleasantly surprised to hear responses I've received from girls ages thirteen to thirty when asked what they want from their dads when it comes to spiritual influence. They said:

- "I like it when my dad calls me to let me know he's thinking of me or praying for me."
- "I really like praying together."
- "I like going to church together or going to a Christian concert."
- "I like it when my dad asks about my relationship with God or encourages me to pray."
- "I wish that we could get more one-on-one time just to talk through things that are going on in my life, questions I have, and emotions I'm dealing with."
- "I wish that my dad would ask me about my spiritual walk, and if I say I'm not doing well, that he would tell me how I can go about fixing it."

I put this spiritual decoding tool last because a daughter will be more open to listening to her dad's input about spiritual matters if he has first laid a relational foundation with her, as noted in the first five tips.

I want to close by clearly sharing my heart so you don't have to decode what I'm saying! I believe in the transformative, healing power of a dad's love expressed through consistent pursuit of his daughter's heart. From my heart to yours, I celebrate men like you who are actively investing in your daughter's life by being in it to win it while being willing to learn. And for you men's ministry leaders, I salute you because you are doing a great service to men, the church, and the world by equipping those you serve to be involved dads, especially with their daughters. Thank you, dads, for helping to change the world … one daughter at a time.

20

MINISTERING TO MEN IN ADDICTION CRISIS

(DANIEL L. WOBSCHALL)

Dan Wobschall is regional director for Be Broken Ministries (Bebroken.com), which is based in San Antonio, Texas. Dan spent thirty-two years in public safety as an EMT and 911 dispatcher. He is an author, speaker, and mentor nationwide to men in the arena of sexual integrity and marriage. Contact him at Dan@Bebroken.com.

A man walks up to me in church on a Sunday morning. He is clearly fearful and embarrassed. He tells me, in a muted voice, that if he doesn't speak to me this morning, his wife is going to leave him over his struggle with pornography. This happened in the church sanctuary with many people within earshot of our conversation.

This type of story is quite common for those who minister to men in crisis and addiction. The wife often recognizes the crisis while the man wallows in his addiction, unaware he needs help. One day she confronts him. She threatens to leave. Ripped out of his cocoon of denial, he comes to me seeking counsel. In many cases (including the one I cited above), the man is a long-time friend or colleague.

Pornography use and addiction is rampant in our society today. A 2014 study from the Barna Group found that 63 percent of US men ages eighteen to thirty use pornography *at least several times a week*. Among thirty-one- to forty-nine-year-olds, the number is 38 percent, and among men over fifty it's 25 percent. The actual numbers are probably even higher, since men tend to underreport undesirable behaviors to pollsters.

Porn rewires the pathways in a man's brain. Men addicted to pornography experience real physical and psychological symptoms during use and after they stop using. These include depression, erectile dysfunction, physical withdrawal symptoms, moodiness, isolation, shame, and fear. Depending on the severity of the addiction, medical intervention may be needed. (I'm not a doctor, so if I recognize a concern I always refer the man to an appropriate medical professional.)

Does this frighten you? Have you abandoned any hope of ministering to this enormous group of men? You shouldn't be afraid. Here are some truths, tools, and insights that can help you minister to a man in the crisis of addiction. Keep in mind these are tools for *crisis* mode and not all of them will be required further down the restoration path.

ASK STRATEGIC QUESTIONS

Specific, well-thought-out questions invite a man to slowly peel back the smelly onion, exposing it to the fresh air of truth. Start with, "How are you?" This may seem like a trivial question, but it's not. The man probably feels terrible about himself. Everyone cares about his wife, but nobody seems to care about him. By asking about him, you demonstrate God's unconditional love, proving that you have not rejected him.

Keep asking questions. Here are a few examples:

- What was life like at home growing up?
- What was your relationship with your parents like?
- Did you ever experience any verbal, sexual, or physical abuse?
- What's your relationship with Christ like?
- How long have you struggled with porn (or other sexual strongholds)?
- Does anyone else know of your struggle?
- Do you think you have a problem with porn?
- Do you masturbate?
- How often do you masturbate?

- Do you want to be free from your addiction/bondage?
- Have you been fully open with your wife about the problem?
- Is another woman involved? (If yes, that needs to end at once!)

Avoid *why* questions, such as, "Why do you keep using porn?" The most common answer to this question is, "I don't know," which shuts down the conversation.

"Why so many questions?" you ask. *Statements harden the heart, but questions prick the conscience.* Simply put, questions make a man think, moving him down the path of self-discovery of truths he has willingly denied or not accepted. Self-discovered truths change the heart. As a friend, minister, or mentor, you need to ask tough questions—questions that make both of you a bit uncomfortable.

Jesus was the master at asking tough questions. He used tough, probing questions to cut right to the heart of the matter.

BE A GOOD LISTENER

In addiction crisis ministry, listening is probably the most valuable skill you can possess. Here are some tips.

Take notes. I recommend making actual handwritten notes as your counselee speaks. This practice enhances recall and clarity of thought as you record it. Refer to your notes before each meeting. Keep your notes private so they cannot be seen by others.

Make eye contact. This man who is opening to you, coming to you for help for a crisis in his life, needs to know you are fully engaged and paying attention.

Learn to read body language. What you hear the man say and what his body language tells you is vital. You need to hear what is *not* being said.

Don't be afraid of silence. As you speak, don't feel the need to fill in silence. Ask a question and then be quiet. Let him think. A long pause in the conversation may end with a breakthrough revelation.

If you feel something has been left out, probe deeper. People in general, and men in particular, will leave out the most painful parts of their story for a variety of reasons. Stress can fog the mind and make it forget. Men feel ashamed, so they hide their sin. Some critical details that need to come to the surface may be too painful or embarrassing to recall.

A skilled listener will hear what's missing and learn to ask important questions that can be critical to the initial decompression stages of a man's immediate crisis. The answers, pleasant or not, give a perspective that helps the man—and you—maneuver your way through the first critical hours or days of confronting the crisis.

It's important to listen well with a man who is in crisis the first time he comes to you or you're not likely to get a second chance.

SHOW TOUGH LOVE

Tough love may sound like a cliché, but in addiction crisis ministry, it's a must. Most men in addiction crisis mode have become good at minimizing or justifying thoughts, words, and behaviors. It's become a twisted version of a safe place. You are not helping a man when you avoid confronting his bad choices. Sugarcoating his lying and deception is a dangerous form of enabling. The man in crisis has been living outside healthy boundaries. If he has come to you for help, then you have the permission and responsibility to reintroduce his life and soul to protective boundaries.

Insist on honesty. Every man I mentor, in crisis or not, hears this statement from me: "One thing I will not tolerate is being lied to. Lie to me once and grace is extended. Lie to me a second time and I'm likely done." Does this seem harsh? A man in crisis needs emotional, rational, relational, and psychological CPR, not Band-Aid pleasantries. Distinguishing between genuine confusion and outright lies takes wisdom, grace, and patience.

The tough-love process might be called *intensive mentoring*. How long the man is in crisis mode must be evaluated on a case-by-case basis. The longer he's been in addiction's grip, the more profound the crisis may last. Here are other factors that affect the crisis timeline:

- Circumstances surrounding the onset of the crisis
- The man's family situation
- Other addictions he may suffer with

- Any legal issues included in the crisis (any potential criminal charges)
- Loss of a job
- Other people affected, besides immediate family (in the case of an affair)
- Any drugs and or alcohol involved
- Whether or not his wife has moved out or asked him to move out

Men in addiction—and that includes addiction to alcohol, drugs, sex, gambling, and so on—often grapple with conflicting thoughts and beliefs. They are likely to contradict themselves in speech and behavior. Their lives have been lived in duplicity, and keeping their facts straight is challenging at best.

As you take your next step in addiction crisis ministry, keep this truth in mind: *Until the man you're ministering to is being honest with himself, he will not be honest with you.* A man who lies to himself will not trust himself and thereby is not likely to trust anyone else. Expect the truth from him and be completely honest with him. In short, speak truth in firm love.

Jesus offers us a powerful weapon in this fight: truth. In John 8:32, the Lord proclaims, "Then you will know the truth, and the truth shall set you free." I've seen dozens of men freed from their addictions when they finally embraced the truth about themselves, their addictions, and the God who loves them still. There is no freedom apart from the truth.

21

CONQUERING PORN ADDICTION

(TODD BURES)

Todd Bures serves on Man to Man Ministries in Victoria, Texas, under the leadership of Glen Dry. Man to Man disciples men into the spiritual leaders God calls them to be. Visit mantomanonline.org for more information.

What's the biggest addiction problem in our world today. Drugs? Alcohol? Not even close. It's pornography. Here are the facts:

- More than 70 percent of men ages eighteen to thirty-four visit a pornography website each month.[1]
- In the US, almost fourteen billion dollars a year is spent on pornography.[2]
- One out of every five mobile-device searches is pornographic.[3]
- Among Christians, 64 percent of men and 15 percent of women view pornography at least once a month.[4]
- At least 93 percent of boys and 62 percent of girls have been exposed to pornography by the age of eighteen.[5]

Why are so many men addicted to pornography? It's cheap. It's easy to get. And it's everywhere. And it stimulates an area of the brain that gives a person a natural high. God intended for this high to be experienced in marriage, but the devil knows how to exploit this feeling and turn it into addiction.

Since 70 percent of men eighteen to thirty-four view pornography monthly, we can assume most of the men we interact with have viewed pornography in the past thirty days. How do we get men to open and admit their struggles? First, what not to do:

- Don't turn holier than thou and start pointing out all his faults.
- Don't start rattling off Bible verses to point out his sin.
- Don't confront him in front of others, especially his family.

The easiest way to get a man to open up about anything is to admit your own struggles. Even if you haven't used pornography, you've probably struggled with sexual lust. Be honest. Provide opportunities to meet in smaller groups where men are more likely to open up with a few trusted individuals, rather than standing up in front of a larger group and admitting their problems.

Be open and honest with men and earn their trust. Allow them to voice their struggles, where they are in their lives and their thoughts, without casting judgment. Once I listen to men, I go into my story. I start with how I first viewed pornography at age twelve, eventually looking at it daily; how I thought it was a secret, even though God knows everything; how I was eventually convicted by the Holy Spirit; and where I am now. It gives hope to the men I talk with that they can conquer that demon too. I don't immediately reveal strategies for beating the addiction. Instead, I let them see the freedom I now enjoy. In most cases, they ask, "How did you do it?" That question is the first step in recovery.

A man must want to change for change to occur. Amid my addiction, I considered myself a good person; therefore, I didn't want to change. Eventually, I went through some difficult issues with my family. I hit a low point. That brokenness led me to seek forgiveness, and only then was I convicted by Christ to look at my own sin. Once a man is convicted to change and reaches out for help, the door will open to help him overcome his addiction.

I tell men the only way to defeat their demons is through faith in Christ. First Corinthians 6:18–20 is a great place to start:

> Flee from sexual immorality. All other sins a person commits are outside the body, but whoever sins sexually, sins against their own body. Do you not know that your bodies are temples of the Holy Spirit, who is in you, whom you have received from God? You are not your own; you were bought at a price. Therefore, honor God with your bodies.

Matthew 5:27–28 explains how lust is the same as adultery; Hebrews 2:18 and 1 Corinthians 10:13 teach us how to deal with temptations. We cannot control our every thought, but we can control what we view and how we respond. God is faithful in his Word, and the Bible gives us plenty of hope. I challenge you to seek out other verses that warn of sexual impurity and help men flee temptation, and how we are to think on things that are pure, lovely, and admirable.

Another step to overcoming addiction is prayer. Be specific with your prayers. Ask God to remove the lustful thoughts and heal the mind and heart of the men in your charge. Pray with them Philippians 4:6–7: "Do not be anxious about anything, but in every situation, by prayer and petition, with thanksgiving, present your requests to God. And the peace of God, which transcends all understanding, will guard your hearts and your minds in Christ Jesus" (ESV).

Teach your men to confess their sins to God and to each other, asking for forgiveness. John tells us, "If we confess our sins, he is faithful and just to forgive us our sins and to cleanse us from all unrighteousness" (1 John 1:9 ESV). I learned when dealing with some issues with my family that forgiveness is a major key to recovering. If you do not repent of your sin, how can you move on? Most times in the process of seeking forgiveness, God will reveal other things in your life and give further conviction to draw you closer to him.

Finally, daily accountability will help you put on the full armor of God and stay on the path of righteousness. I have two close friends, Toby and Tyson, with whom I have regular accountability. I encourage an accountability group of three men. Ecclesiastes 4:12 tells us that "though a man might prevail against one who is alone, two will withstand him—a threefold cord is not quickly broken." Through an accountability of three, if one stumbles, the other two can flank him, lift him up, and carry him through the rough spots. There are also helpful tools out there like Covenant Eyes to help with accountability.

You may also want to keep a private list of men who have faced and defeated this demon. This is not for public disclosure, but as a reminder of God's faithfulness. Used with permission, those testimonies can give strength and hope to men seeking to change. In the process, you may also discover opportunities to connect accountability partners.

Help men recognize their own weaknesses and be aware of where and when they might be tempted. Sometimes the solution is as simple as driving down a different road or limiting access to the computer. Here are some additional recommendations to share with your men in recovery:

- Do not get on the Internet alone. Go online only in the family room or when others are home.
- Have an accountability partner set passwords for computer and phone settings, blocking access to inappropriate content.
- If certain television shows cause your mind to wander, stop watching them.
- Delete social media if you are tempted by the content.
- You may have to make the hard choice and leave some friendships or other relationships.

This addiction is not easily seen by others; however, God sees our hearts. We must guard our hearts and beat the addiction. The best way to have men admit the addiction is through honest communication. Once the lines of communication are open, explain the reason for addiction, discuss faith in Christ, and stress prayer and accountability. With God's help, the addiction can be broken and the lustful nature removed.

22

REACHING MEN ON THE FRINGE

(KEVIN BURKE)

Kevin Burke is a discipling consultant with Lutheran Men in Mission, responsible for training men's ministry specialists and networking ministry leaders across the US. He continues to help grow and lead the ecumenical group Project Twelve. Find out more at lutheranmeninmission.org and projecttwelve.net.

"All means all." We recite this phrase often in our church. Not because we practice it perfectly, but because we constantly fall short.

To love and include *all* means to break down barriers and open doors. We strive to demonstrate respect and allow others to have and even share their opinions. People experience life and see things in different ways, but we can't say *all means all* if we don't invite them to the table. We can't expect our invitation to be accepted unless we have established a relationship and built trust.

How do we define "the fringe"? Someone beyond our standards or expectations? Is it a unit of measurement set by society? Is it set by the Bible? If so, Old Testament? New Testament? Western translation or Eastern?

Often people on the fringe feel as if they cannot be heard. Or perhaps worse, they feel they are heard and are ostracized because of what they say or how they present themselves. In many cases, an individual may have values virtually identical to most of the members of your men's group, but he simply *feels* like an outsider. In other cases, he is wrestling with unrepentant sin in his life, trying to sort out right from wrong. Of course, Romans 3:23 confirms, "All have sinned and fall short of the glory of God." But as a church, do we exclude some sinners more than others? Are there sins that would prevent you from inviting another man to the table? Those who steal, covet, or commit adultery? What about murder?

I worked as a prison guard at a maximum-security prison in Texas for six years. Five of those years, I was assigned to the psych department. Imagine the worst of the worst. Now add the encumbrance of mental illness. I spent those years outnumbered by men who, beyond all reasonable doubt, had taken another's life. It was only after I moved and left the prison system that I could grasp the idea of forgiveness. It was only by looking back that I had any inkling of God's love for those men. If Christ died for me, he died for them as well.

At times, it sounds noble to speak of visiting prisoners, serving food to the homeless, and tending to the widows and orphans of our world. Can we honestly say we serve not only because *our* identity is in Christ but because *their* identity is in Christ?

We can decide with great intellectual conviction that all men are invited and welcome. But that will never really happen *unless we also love*. We can expend great amounts of energy on barbecues, sport and music outreaches, and planning impressive events. But the most effective tool we have for drawing men into the body of Christ is our love for each other. Jesus said, "By this everyone will know that you are my disciples, if you love one another" (John 13:35). In other words, if we want to reach men, we need first to touch hearts.

It's also worth remembering that we can thoughtfully invite and warmly love, but there will still be those who don't feel welcome. Never forget, anyone who views himself as an outsider *is* an outsider. If you are committed to reaching these men, then you must also commit to affirming their feelings.

One of the great challenges of ministry is to *validate* a man's feelings while encouraging him to hold those feelings in check and *take a chance* with your group. A wise strategy is to come alongside him. Without overwhelming him with detail, confess your own brokenness. Acknowledge that we all come with our own baggage, even though it may not be evident on the surface. Share stories, not necessarily describing how men have experienced amazing conversions, but stories of men from different backgrounds and personal challenges who have found a connection with God and with each other. Humbly add that some of these men have even found a church home or a safe place within your group. If you can help a man on the fringe see that we are all in need and all *different*, then you have opened his heart and mind to the possibility that we are all the *same* in the eyes of God.

You probably don't want to claim, "I know exactly how you feel." But you can suggest, "There are men in our group who have been through the same kind of experience." Can you see the subtle difference? You're first job is to listen, and to listen well.

Next, you'll want to say, "Thank you for sharing with me." You may be tempted to follow up with words like "but …" or "you're wrong" or some kind of deflection. But please hold your tongue. This isn't about you, it's about them and helping them open their lives to the God of love, hope, righteousness, and forgiveness.

Finally, check your motives. Don't seek out men on the fringe—or any man—with the goal of "saving them" or convincing them to join your church. Your motive should be relationship for the sake of relationship. As soon as you enter in with an expectation, you're setting yourself and your new friend up for failure. Plus, there is the likelihood that you will not agree with some of their core values or life strategies. Many of those on the fringe—those with whom you are trying to connect—will be on the fringe for a reason. Have you developed the skill to communicate and listen to someone who is almost your opposite in the way they look, think, speak, and feel?

The list of possible differences is long, beginning with race, nationality, and mental or physical disabilities. Can you imagine yourself as an individual in one of these categories on the outside looking in at your ministry group? Do you unintentionally discriminate against men in a different income bracket or with a different marital status? Let's not move on without addressing discrimination against millennials, the LGBTQ community, men with tattoos and piercings, or guys with different political views.

There are also the "nones" and the "dones." The "nones" are individuals who have no affiliation with the church. They weren't raised in the church, didn't go to Sunday school, do not know the lingo, and may not have any clue on how to look up a passage of Scripture. That doesn't mean they lack compassion. They are called to help and serve others. They just don't do it with a Christian marker. They have a great curiosity about faith but question the need of a religious institution to do good deeds. Plus, they are confused or put off by phrases like "born again" or "led by the Spirit."

"Dones" have left the church—maybe with good reason. We need to be sensitive to their history with religion. What if a man was sexually abused by a member of the clergy? Can you blame him for putting space between himself and the very people who were supposed to keep him safe? Every man has a story, and we may never be part of his inner circle to hear what he has gone through. Acknowledge things not known, and be okay with what is not said. Many "dones" were also burnt out. They could have been a part of the 10 percent of individuals who did all the work in their last men's group. Their time and passion were taken advantage of, and they couldn't do that forever. Their faith may still be strong, but they no longer want the burden that seems to come with church affiliation.

For better or for worse, each one of us comes to the table with our own past and experiences. A man who has bitterness or anger for a reason has that right. Opinions belong to each one of us. I can't tell a man his feelings are wrong. I may feel the opposite and that's my right, but that doesn't change the fact that we are each children of God. On Sunday, I will be shoulder to shoulder taking communion with men who are different from me. And that's a good thing.

Each one of us has our time and season. If I had been turned away when I truly needed someone, I would have been done with the church. The contrast is true. When I was struggling the most, that was when I was welcomed and reassured of my place in the fold. The shepherd sought after the one lost sheep. That's often how it works.

Creating a welcoming atmosphere begins with church leadership and needs to be top of mind for all staff and volunteers. First-timers, seekers, and new invitees should feel no pressure or judgment. They are people, not projects. Let's certainly not expect them to break down, unburden their souls, and be transformed on their first visit. If God wants to orchestrate that turn of events, awesome. But please don't put that expectation on any human.

Relationships are not based on ulterior motives. We are called to disciple and walk in the ditches with our brothers in Christ. It's easy to talk about discipling in a church classroom, but what about when you are wakened by a 2:00 a.m. phone call? Are you willing to get into the crap of life with them then? As a friend and pastoral leader, do these men know they can call you anytime, for anything? As difficult as that is, that's the goal. Once you've acquired that awesome bond, you know it. It's the I'd-walk-through-fire-wearing-gasoline-boxers-for-you type of bond (an actual quote from a men's retreat).

Discipling men begins with loving each man and treating him like the child of God that he is. It should not matter who he is or what he has done. That's how you earn the right to share your faith. I hope you'll join me as I try to live with no regrets, gaining a reputation for treating all others as image bearers of God. If we truly love and respect our neighbor, how can they feel like they are on the fringe?

23

OVERCOMING RACIAL AND CULTURAL BARRIERS TO DISCIPLE MEN

(ELMO WINTERS)

Reverend Elmo Winters has worked as a church planter, pastor, Bible institute instructor, and short-term missionary to Kenya, Mexico, Russia, and Israel. He is the executive director of The Kingdom Group International, LLC, and works to bring racial and cultural reconciliation and unity throughout the world. He holds an MBA and has authored the soul-winning book *Growing by Going*. Contact him at kingdomgroup .co or e-mail elmow1@att.net.

One of the most difficult challenges in discipling men is reaching guys of varying racial and cultural diversities. This is even more evident when it comes to white men and their African-American counterparts.

Caucasian men often say, "I really want to reach out to my black brothers, but I don't know how." Complicating this issue is mistrust that many men of color harbor against other men who don't look like them. At the core of these concerns are questions of sincerity and common ground. Invisible walls inhibit the development of any sincere relationships that have the potential to promote making disciples of all men, regardless of their differences.

But there are ways to overcome many of these obstacles. Admittedly, some situations are more difficult than others. There are no easy answers. Prayer for guidance from the Holy Spirit is always the ultimate necessity for success in overcoming racial and cultural barriers in discipling men.

Change begins in the heart. Proverbs 4:23 says, "Keep thy heart with all diligence, for out of it are the issues of life" (KJV). It's significant that one of the meanings of the original word for *issues* in this verse refers to borders. This innermost part of man—the heart—serves as the gatekeeper for much of what we do. Our hearts govern our motivation for going beyond ourselves to reach out to others. How many times have we heard, "If your heart is not in it, you will not do it, or it will not last"? Admittedly, if the heart is not ready for a relationship with another man who is different from himself, even if begun with the best intentions, it will not be meaningful or last long.

Any man seeking to build a bridge across racial and cultural lines must first ask himself this question: *Do I really want to have this relationship?* A man must undergo a thorough and serious search of his heart to determine genuine motivation and sincerity.

A man who wants to connect with brothers of different races cannot be subconsciously fighting the American Civil War, filled with prejudice and the ideas of racial superiority. Nor can he be bound up in the mental slavery of the old Southern plantations. These are real issues of the heart that must be spiritually and permanently dealt with. If not, they will always be hindrances to building fellowship and discipling men who are diverse.

The Word of God directs us to Christ for the remedy for this type of heart problem. Romans 10:10 explains, "For with the heart man believeth unto righteousness; and with the mouth confession is made unto salvation" (KJV). Christ is the only one who can deliver us from the worldly bias and prejudices that too often shape our lives from infancy to adulthood. Jesus alone can heal the pain associated with bigotry and hatred. When he changes a man's heart, he changes the man's life and teaches him to love his neighbor as he loves himself.

Kingdom Group International and Gulf South Men of Louisiana

conducted a survey to determine what characteristics were most valuable in successful relationships that crossed racial and cultural lines. Among those surveyed, 48 percent of the men said working together with common interests and shared values was the number one component in these relationships.

Men are passionate about some of the same things, regardless of the color of their skin. Men love sports, hunting, and fishing. Some take pride in building things while others love blowing up stuff. Many men love cooking, and all men enjoy eating, especially relishing foods their wives would not approve.

One powerful way to break down barriers is to invite diverse men to work together on a project that involves one of these activities. This should be something that requires equal "hands-on" participation and interdependency, where there is reliance on each other. The activity must highlight the value of every man involved and occasionally include opportunities for shared leadership. No man should feel less than any other, and all must gain a sense of camaraderie. Building mutual respect and appreciation is key to reaching across racial and cultural barriers.

Another important ingredient for effectively discipling diverse men is Christ-centeredness. One-third of the men responding to the survey believed that the success of their multiracial relationships was based in part on their connections with Christ. He is the invisible glue that holds them together, even when they differ, especially along denominational lines.

Men who love the Lord find common ground in his love and compassion for all people. Often, this love serves as the catalyst for working together on community projects and church activities. Being rooted in Christ is essential in erasing any sense of racial superiority, as well as helping men rebound from feelings of inferiority. All men are made equal in Christ, as the apostle Paul writes in Galatians 3:28: "There is neither Jew nor Greek, there is neither bond nor free, there is neither male nor female: for ye are all one in Christ Jesus" (KJV).

Hosting small-group meetings that include varying races and cultures often facilitates relationship building for discipling men. The focus must be on Christ and his teachings. Worldly issues or politics should be avoided unless they tie into the study. Hot-topic discussions should be dodged as well, except in cases where diversity brings better understanding and unity. Divisive matters rarely enhance relationships, especially among those seeking to tear down walls of separation. Remember, as believers we are instructed: "Through the peace that ties you together, do your best to maintain the unity that the Spirit gives" (Ephesians 4:3 GW).

One of the most challenging prerequisites for discipling men who are ethnically diverse is the willingness to accept their differences without being judgmental or critical. Sharing customs and cultures of all races of men can provide an intriguing and rewarding experience, while at the same time building shared respect, trust, and humility. Men who feel respected are more likely to participate. *Being different is a matter of nature; being accepted and admired because of these differences is a matter of choice.*

Think about how boring any relationship would be if all men were alike. One thing that helps build strong groups among men is a heightened level of admiration for one another. This is where each person recognizes and finds worth in some characteristic of every member of the group, not based on prejudices or preconceived notions, but on acknowledging the value of including men with a wide variety of backgrounds and cultures.

The value of trust in relationship building cannot be overemphasized. Without it, no initiative to attract men of all cultures can succeed. In fact, the lack of trust is a major barrier when it comes to bringing African-American men together with Caucasian men. Distrust arises when men cite negative past experiences with men of other races. Too often men question whether one side or the other can truly be counted on to keep their word or fulfill the commitment that has been made.

Oftentimes, black men think most white men really do not care about them and simply *go through the motions*, or pretend they care whenever they reach out to have any relationship. The question they ask is, "Why should I trust you now? You never cared before." In response, many white men respond by overcompensating for past injustices, which does little to solve the problem. This simply drives lack of trust deeper into the minds of their African-American counterparts. It is not until both sides come together and genuinely put their histories behind them that a fulfilling and meaningful union can be forged. No one can change what happened yesterday; if men focus on the past, they cannot move successfully into the future.

None of this can be achieved without a spirit of humility. Those reaching across barriers, as well as the recipients of their efforts, must demonstrate humility. Unity will be enhanced as humble men acknowledge their mutual brokenness and need for a Savior.

The obstacles to discipling men of varying ethnicities is huge, but the benefits and rewards of overcoming these obstacles can be extraordinary. I salute any sincere and thoughtful effort to bridge the gap that exists between men who desire to develop fulfilling relationships with one another. Commit to a genuine goal of uniting all men, regardless of their differences, and a discipling relationship can flourish. Get guys to work together toward a common interest. Be willing and eager to accept each other's uniqueness, tempered by trust and humility. That builds a powerful foundation for unity in Christ.

Now go and overcome those barriers that hinder making disciples of all men!

24

MINISTERING TO HUSBANDS AND FATHERS BEHIND BARS

(MIKE BEHAR)

Mike Behar is an ordained pastor through Abundant Life Family Ministries in Ocala, Florida. He is certified as a men's ministry leader through Man in the Mirror Leadership Training Center, and he is an ordained chaplain with the International Fellowship of Chaplains. Mike and his wife, Wendy, are the founders and directors of Unlimited Discipleship Ministries, which has a primary focus on marriage discipleship. Mike currently teaches a weekly men's Bible study called "The Man Cave" and ministers to men at Marion Correctional Institute.

My wife, Wendy, and I have been involved in marriage and family ministry for more than fifteen years, and we've seen some tough situations. For example, when a solider comes home after a lengthy deployment, the adjustment is sometimes too much to bear. We've counseled couples through addictions, adultery, and even physical abuse. But the most amazing lessons—and success stories—have come after we were invited to bring our marriage ministry to Florida's Marion Correctional Institute (MCI), the third largest maximum-security prison in the country.

Imagine when a man is incarcerated for ten or fifteen years, meeting his children for the first time or attempting to step into the leadership role as husband and father. The divorce rate in these situations is almost 100 percent. It was the first time in the history of MCI that a Christian group had been granted approval to minister to the men on the *inside* while the wives of the incarcerated men were ministered to on the *outside*.

We joined forces with a prison ministry called Xtreme Soulutions, run by founder Blaine Whitt. I wasn't sure what to expect, but after my first meeting with a group of fifteen prisoners, I was sure God had the wrong man for the job.

I had no idea how to share the gospel with convicted felons in maximum-security lockup. But I figured I better shoot straight, so I humbly began with my personal testimony. "Except for the grace of God," I said, "I would be sitting where you are."

I told them about my father, and how I grew up hating him, which led to a life of drugs, rebellion, and extreme anger. My wife and I had experienced the devastation and pain of unwanted divorces. Even though Wendy and I loved each other, we learned that love wasn't enough. We both brought truckloads of issues into our marriage and continually stepped on "land mines," those buried hurts that unexpectedly blow up in your face.

As the prisoners began to share about their relationships, I was shocked to hear them refer to the women in their lives as "baby mommas." They said things like, "I have four children by three different baby mommas." My heart was torn by the dysfunction of broken relationships. I imagined the hundreds of children who had no relationship with their incarcerated biological fathers. How could I help these men overcome their dishonoring of women and their lack of responsibility?

MINISTERING TO MARRIAGES IN CRISIS

As a launching point, we began to look at God's purpose for marriage. God did not make marriage about love, but about removing aloneness. God in his sovereignty created him (Adam) with aloneness needs and her (Eve) with different aloneness needs. His plan was for husbands and wives to serve each other and meet these needs.

We broke open God's Word and slowly began to explain God's

plan of redemption. We told them that even though they had made mistakes, God still loved them and wanted to turn into good what satan meant for destruction.

Many of the men had a hard time acknowledging they had needs. After years of going without their needs being met, they had pretty much given up any dreams of living a fulfilling life. Living with constantly dashed hopes was just too painful. But we could see small breakthroughs when the men realized that the women in their lives were going through the same thing. Their women also had unmet needs—needs their incarcerated men might someday be able to fill.

One of the best tools for breaking through the hardened hearts of these men was to be honest about my own vulnerabilities. A good friend once told me, "If all I share with you are my strengths, my victories, and my champion moments, I build a wall between us; but when I'm willing to share my failures, weaknesses, and my shortcomings, then I build a bridge between us. I become relatable."

Once the bridges are built, God allows us to speak some challenging truths into the lives of others. As I share my testimony—complete with lessons learned the hard way and biblical truth learned through consistent study—I'm careful to never come across in a condescending or condemning way.

STRAIGHT TALK ABOUT ROMANCE

Helping men understand intimacy needs and how men and women define the same need differently can be a lot of fun. Men appreciate honest talk about sexuality, and there's no reason to get excessively graphic as you speak because they pick up what you're talking about quickly.

Women define affection as holding hands, looking into one another's eyes, and talking. And guys? Well, we most often see affection as sexual touching—and it is best when she initiates. It's surprising how many men don't know that intimacy is a gift to be received, not taken by force, intimidation, or expectation. I tell them, "A need taken never satisfies."

Most often, men who are incarcerated have been conditioned to be takers, leaving damaged women and family members in their wake. I have seen men come to a place of true repentance as they realize the mistakes they've made and come to understand their needs are real and God intended for their needs to be met. As we discuss the three dimensions of intimacy—spirit, soul, and body—we admonish each man to be the leader, not dominator, of his home.

SPIRITUAL LEADERSHIP

Many men believe that as long as we work hard and bring home a paycheck, our job is done. Sure, our wives appreciate it when the bills are paid, when there's a decent roof over our heads, when food is in the cupboard, and when she has a safe car to drive. But real security means so much more than providing physical necessities.

The idea that men are supposed to be spiritual leaders in the home is uncharted territory for most of us. But when men fulfill this role, it brings great reward and a sense of security for our wives. I went through an extended period as a workaholic until Wendy finally told me that we could live in a shack as long as she knew our marriage was on solid ground.

At first I thought she was crazy. Then I heard what she was saying: she needed *emotional* security more than *physical* security. It was a hard lesson for me to learn, but God has helped me learn and apply his principles to meet my wife's need.

EMOTIONAL HEALING

Prison culture says, "Bad things happen, but you just have to suck it up and get over it." But the Bible says, "Blessed are those who mourn, for they will be comforted" (Matthew 5:4). Emotional wounds require a period of mourning and resolution. Only then will we find blessing and comfort. By carrying unresolved wounds, we deny ourselves true intimacy in our marriage relationships.

The most common wound in the lives of incarcerated men is the father wound. Men who grew up abandoned or abused by their fathers often carry deep hurt and issues of unforgiveness. By sharing my own scars, I help prisoners see how my unforgiveness toward my father kept me in captivity far worse than any prison cell. Then I take it a step further by reminding them of the command "to honor your father and mother." It normally gets very quiet in the room as I teach this subject.

One inmate recently told me that even though he has three children by two different women, when he gets released in a year he wants to work at establishing a right relationship with his children. He also desires to be a godly husband to the right woman. He said that God had opened his eyes through our time together, and he wondered aloud why he had never heard the principles we shared. Another man committed to be the spiritual leader God intended for his family.

Working with incarcerated men to heal marriages and family relationships in desperate need of repair is one of the most rewarding areas of ministry I have ever experienced. Every week, I walk out of Marion Correctional Institute feeling totally jazzed.

The men you minister to may not be in a literal prison, but they are probably held captive by something. Resentments, hurts, and anger imprison far more men than the correctional system. Lots of men are separated from their families. They respond to transparency and vulnerability. God is honored when marriage and family are held in high esteem.

Not all men are married, but any ministry to men needs to include an emphasis on respecting, healing, and honoring the sanctity of marriage—even in the toughest situations.

25

HUNTING, FISHING, AND OUTDOOR ADVENTURE MINISTRY IN YOUR CHURCH

(T. J. GREANEY)

T. J. Greaney is an award-winning outdoor, travel, and adventure writer, photographer, and radio show host. He is also founder of Kids Outdoor Zone, the nation's fastest-growing hunting, fishing, and outdoor ministry for men and boys. Find out more at kidsoutdoorzone.com.

Recently, I hosted a men's breakfast at my new church. I sensed these predominantly twentysomething fathers, college-age men, and millennials needed an "experience." We began the morning with bacon and eggs cooked over a campfire, as much as they wanted, on warm tortillas. We set up a .22 caliber gun range and six archery targets with simple Mathews Genesis bows. To finish it off, I brought my throwing axes and four-wheelers. These young men came alive. Many had never done a lot of these activities before, and those who had loved it as a men's ministry activity.

If God has been talking to you about starting an outdoor ministry in your church, then do a few things for confirmation. Pray. Ask Jesus, "Is this my calling and what you want me to do?" Talk to your wife, your friends, your pastor, and your men's ministry leaders. Share your passion and thoughts. Come with some solid ideas, but don't insist you have all the answers. Be willing to be the point person and to commit to do the work. Pastors and church staff are not looking for more work or assignments.

Starting an outdoor ministry at your church does not have to be difficult. First, identify a few guys who want to commit to regular meetings that include outdoor activities and campfire talks that center on Jesus. I would also say don't worry about making it too structured. Anyone who has sat with a brother fishing, at hunting camp, or around a campfire knows what I mean.

Know that usually the pastor or staff won't play a big role. It would surely be helpful to have their support, but give them freedom to opt in or out of the adventures. Of course, a pastor who engages in these type activities with his men gets huge street credit and loyalty among his men. Third, know it might take a while to get it going. God is well known for taking his time when he is creating ministry. Jesus was never in a hurry, so breathe.

Your outings and events do not have to be week-long survival camps or four-day elk hunts. Those events you would plan on the side as a bonus option for those who come to your regular outdoor ministry meetings. One of the most important things to remember when you are planning your time is time. Men don't think they have much of it when it comes to ministry and talking to Jesus. For family men, there are times when kids' baseball, basketball, and youth sports will get in the way. And you need to honor their commitment to family. I recommend you plan your outings for one Saturday a month, and a half Saturday at that. Perhaps, the second Saturday of the month, eight in the morning to noon, rain or shine. Food in the morning with coffee, easy lunch in the afternoons. Make it a no-brainer. Always the same Saturday, always meet and adapt to the weather if need be, but always meet.

Make sure you include an invite that lets the guys who don't have outdoor skills know they are welcomed, even encouraged. So often we guys won't chime in if we feel we can't compete or do not know anything about the topic. We surely don't want to be exposed. Put it in the invite and Sunday overhead graphic, "Never Been Shootin'? Then Come Learn." They all want to come, they all crave it inside, so help them know it is going to be good and they will be fine.

There is nothing better than the palm of your hand to get guys to come out. Yes, that is right—shake hands and invite guys. Make yourself available and offer any information they may request. This is also a good time to show them it's not just a redneck throwdown. I hear that all the time: "Oh, that's those hunting guys up there," or, "It's a bunch of rednecks." Well, yeah, we are both, but there are executives from software companies, other ministry leaders, fathers, a writer, a bookkeeper, and a landscaper too. We all love the outdoors, or we're the guys who didn't grow up outdoors and want to learn. When you go face-to-face with them, they see you are not all that scary after all. Be who you are—you do kill stuff and eat it, but it's okay. This will not be for every guy at your church, so don't be offended. There are lots of ministry opportunities, and this is just one of them. (The best one, but just one.)

Then the question comes up, "So what will we be doing?" This is easy if you plan it in advance. Go to a gun range, go to a fishing pond, invite a game warden or professional angler to come speak. Or just hang out around a campfire and eat a huge breakfast. Whatever you do, there needs to be three key elements: Manliness—guys together doing something that brings in adrenaline or thoughts of adventure. There needs to be food—feed them and allow big servings. No lettuce sandwiches allowed, but bacon, hot dogs with ample fixings, Gatorade, and sweet tea. Of course, you need to bring the message. Don't preach; it's not a Sunday school class, so please spare them the same ole, same ole. Get men to give testimonies, share Wild at Heart elements, get real with them. Go real, and you will get allegiance.

I recommend an element that includes boys, specifically the fatherless. Men who come to church are told that the goal is to become a deacon or Sunday school teacher. Both are good, but they rarely speak to a man's deepest heart issues. Many boys in America do not have dads. Moreover, most boys do little outside, and if they do, it is rarely structured with a godly message or a male mentor. If you are an outdoor guy, it is also important for us to raise up the next generation to carry on the heritage of the outdoors. When you take a boy whose feet have never walked uneven ground into the presence of God through the outdoors, you can change him for a lifetime, for eternity. It is in these moments, this element of your Saturday, where you will be in the presence of the Holy Spirit like you rarely, if ever, experience. Kids Outdoor Zone is a boys' hunting and fishing ministry that offers monthly materials you can use that includes shooting, fishing, survival, and more. There is something new every month, which may provide the structure you need to make the outdoor ministry successful.

You are going to need some gear. It is not uncommon for a few good men who have plenty of gear to be willing to share their guns and fishing rods. When word gets out to the members of your church, you may have offers of land use, gear, and even money, especially if you are mentoring boys.

Note: You don't ever want to base a ministry around the need for money and gear. Yes, you need some things, but too often money changes things and it becomes about the stuff—the deer lease or the hunt club. Keep it simple and know God will provide tons of cool experiences and opportunities if he is at the center.

You may get the high eyebrow from your pastor or the elders at your church when they hear guns will be involved. That usually brings the insurance question. We have found most church insurance policies cover all activities and do not exclude shooting sports and hunting. If there is a question, then talk to the agent and explain the ministry. It rarely has become a problem, and the worst-case scenario is that you add a liability item at a minimal cost, which you and the guys can cover if need be. Make it a nonissue.

If this is your heart, your calling, and if your church is not willing to walk with you in this mission field, then, well, you need to ask yourself a hard question: Is this the right church for me? Blasphemy! Well, no. I have heard guys tell me that their pastor or men's ministry leader told them they "did not do that kind of stuff." Maybe your church has specific ministry ideas and a direction they are going, and this does not fit. Maybe they are against hunting or worried it might offend someone. There are those folks out there. That is the church you are going to right now, so what does that do to your heart? Talk to Jesus, brother.

The legendary John Wayne once said, "Don't put your foot in the stirrup if you are not willing to ride." Jesus was intentional about spending time outdoors. He chose true fishermen to take his message to the world. He went to the woods and mountaintops to talk with his Father. He sat with his most trusted men night after night around campfires in intimate conversation, training, and teaching. Read the end of the book of John and you'll see that Jesus had his last conversation with his closest men around a campfire after they were fishing. I would say that is a pretty good model for ministry—wouldn't you?

26

MINISTERING TO UNEMPLOYED MEN

(PHIL REDDICK)

Phil Reddick is an associate pastor at Briarwood Presbyterian Church (PCA) and has directed the Ministry of Young Business Leaders (YBL) for thirty-three years. YBL is an evangelism, discipleship, and mentoring ministry to men in the marketplace. Their website is ybl.org.

In the Great Recession years of 2008 through 2011, I had several men calling my office and each conversation began the same way: "Phil, can we meet for fifteen minutes or so?" In almost every case, I knew what they wanted—a job.

These men were hoping to network with people who might provide opportunities for employment or re-employment. But even more than a job, they desperately needed a dose of encouragement. So much of a man's self-worth comes from his work. Job loss can destroy a man's self-image, self-confidence, and sense of significance.

During the Great Recession, I listened to many men of high integrity and honorable intentions share stories that went something like this: "My sixteen-year career with my company has come to an end. For the first time in years, I do not have a demanding job where I can be challenged and absorbed for seventy hours each week. Although the process has been abrupt and devastating at some levels, I do not need to ask God why it happened. I know that my commitment to God and his purposes came in second to my career, my financial goals, and my sense of security. I would, however, like to learn where God is taking me and find another job I can embrace with passion."

How would you respond to this man? Tell him he has the wrong perspective? Are employment issues even an appropriate topic for men's ministry?

God made men to work (see Genesis 2:15). Yet many men are unemployed or underemployed—and with automation taking over more jobs, the situation is likely to get even worse. How do we minister to men who do not have work?

FOUR REMINDERS

No matter what the economy, a men's minister or adult ministries pastor is going to interact with men who are dealing with job change, underemployment, and unemployment. You also will be involved in connecting people who are looking for their first "real" job. It goes with the territory.

As I got together with each man, I concentrated on four items: (1) you need to get out of the house; (2) you need to network with others; (3) you need a safe place where you feel loved, appreciated, and affirmed; and (4) you need people who are praying, have you on their minds, and are actively listening to and pursuing potential employers and job openings for you. Let's deal with these one at a time.

You need to get out of the house. Tell him, "Don't let shame box you in. It's very easy to feel discouraged with everyone going to work while you're at home. Don't listen to satan's lies. You are still significant in God's sight. Yet you still need to have places to go and people to be around."

You need to network with others. Keep looking for work. Go out with friends. Finding a job is a numbers game: the more contacts you make, the more likely you are to find employment.

You need a place where you can connect with people, feel safe, and be appreciated. A small group does these things. Plug him into a solid group of committed men where he will receive spiritual nourishment, fellowship, and ongoing prayer. You know how it works. When that man is part of a small group, he will begin building a trust relationship

with other guys. Before long, those new spiritual partners will be offering solid advice, job leads, and references.

You need people who are praying for you. And then model that
prayer. Offer to pray with every job-seeking or discouraged man who
comes into your office. If he says yes, pray right then and there. Spend
time on your own praying for these men too. Your prayers may very
well make all the difference in the world.

One company in town hired half a dozen men in our men's group
for whom I had been praying. Because of their new work schedule,
most of them had to miss our regular men's Bible study. I would kid
them and say, "I'm not going to pray for you to get a job if you're going
to leave the group!"

HOW DO I HELP A MAN
NOT BECOME DISCOURAGED?

Remind him, "You will get another job." Hammer that statement home.
No matter how long it takes, tell him, "You will find work." This one
statement gave a friend of mine (who had been out of work for over a
year) tremendous hope through the whole process.

Give him a *workable schedule*. One of the most frequent questions
I'll ask is, "What does your day look like?" Then I'll follow up with,
"Do you spend all your time looking and connecting? What about
time alone with God, time with your family, exercise? Are you taking
time to do anything fun?" These are all relevant questions.

My experience is that most men won't fill all their time with a job
search. They should treat looking for a job as their new job, but that
means trying to keep as "normal" a schedule as possible. It can also be
a time of blessing as he spends more time with family, helps with the
kids' homework, and gets in shape. Encourage him to pursue hobbies
or interests that might result in starting his own business or changing
careers. Also encourage him to:

- Be thankful for where God has placed him
- Be more engaged with friends, write letters, and make
  phone calls
- Do something fun every second or third day

A SUGGESTED DAY

Morning:

- Get up at a set time in the morning and work out.
- Spend time with the Lord in prayer, Bible study, and meditation.
- Check the Internet for job openings and for responses from companies for which you have reached out.
- Eat lunch with someone, or invite someone over for soup and a sandwich.

Afternoon:

- Check the Internet again or read up on current opportunities.
- Practice new job skills or become more proficient in the skills you possess.
- Offer to help pick up the kids, help with homework, or play ball in the yard.

Evening:

- Help with dinner or the cleanup.
- Be present with your family.
- Communicate and listen to God, your spouse, and your kids.
- Read business journals.
- Research companies for which you have applied or to which you will apply.
- Relax.
- Go to bed at a reasonable hour.

SERVING YOUR UNEMPLOYED BROTHER

Make it a priority to meet regularly with those who are unemployed. Recommend a few books or passages of Scripture that offer encouragement. Find other guys to join you who are willing to help too. Many have experienced the same or a similar situation. Helping others find employment is a wonderful way to glorify God and serve others.

If the conversation moves to "Why did this happen?" remind him that God's infinite love for him sometimes involves adversity. Remind him that almost every great man of God had a time of testing in the desert—and each one of them emerged stronger from it. God uses this method to direct, to discipline, to develop, and to give us an eternal perspective. Have him look up passages such as: "Rejoice in hope, be patient in tribulation, be constant in prayer" (Romans 12:12 ESV) and "For the moment all discipline seems painful rather than pleasant, but later it yields the peaceful fruit of righteousness to those who have been trained by it" (Hebrews 12:11 ESV).

Embolden him to not let this event pass without seeking God and discovering what he wants to teach him. *How can God be glorified in this situation? How can I point others to him?* Look at these passages:

"For I know the plans I have for you," declares the LORD, "plans for welfare and not for evil, to give you a future and a hope." (Jeremiah 29:11)

Always being prepared to make a defense to anyone who asks you for a reason for the hope that is in you; yet do it with gentleness and respect. (1 Peter 3:15 ESV)

Above all, do not let men get isolated. Satan loves to make us feel like we are all alone and there is no way out. Be creative in spending time with him: over lunch, by grabbing a cup of coffee or hitting golf balls, or as a jogging partner. Text him, e-mail him, leave a voicemail. It is essential he knows this is a temporary circumstance, you are his teammate, and you will not give up on him.

OUR GOD REIGNS

God has got this. He is in control. He has a purpose. Tell those men who are feeling broken not to worry about what others think. This is between him, the Lord, and his family. Listen, learn, grow! Bless the God of heaven by faith. Rejoice always. Have a grateful heart. Reach out to others. Love your neighbor.

Keep repeating the statement, "You will find another job." We don't know God's timing, but we do know this season that feels like a desert can actually be overflowing with opportunities for a man to try new experiences, grow in his trust and faith in God, and even be a blessing to his family, friends, and faith-based charities. He could be an invaluable resource—and it may be his next job.

God has created us to be workers. God worked in creation and his Holy Spirit is still working on our sanctification. This is preparation for the future. Not only are we workers here on earth, but we will also be workers in heaven.

27

MINISTRY TO MILLENNIALS, YOUNG MEN, AND THE NEXT GENERATION

(DAVID GREGG)

David Gregg is a pastor in California, as well as the regional director for Christian Service Brigade, an eighty-year-old discipleship ministry, and he also serves as managing editor for *Valor Magazine*. For more information, visit csbministries.org.

How do we reach young men for Christ? The same way we always have: by personally discipling them. Older men are uniquely gifted to do this work. Men are designed by God to take dominion through ordering, building, and beautifying. We are designed to lead, fight, struggle, and enjoy the process. And these are the very drives and skills it takes to minister to young men.

As you prepare your older or more experienced men for this important work, it is essential to communicate that it is Christ who has *called them* and *equipped them* for this ministry of discipleship. If Christ does the work, it will not fail.

MINISTRY TO YOUNG MEN TAKES FAITH

A friend of mine was an older father to a difficult fourteen-year-old son. He worked hard at his job and came home tired but would still spend hours in his orchard trimming and pruning. One day I asked him, "Brother, why do you spend so much time in your garden and yet you spend so little time investing in the garden of your son's heart?" After a moment of deep contemplation, he looked up at me, then pointed to a row of well-manicured fruit trees. "Because I know I can make a difference out there."

My friend had lost faith because he had *misplaced* his faith, placing it in his son instead of in the God who does miracles. Encourage your men to see young men with eyes of faith as they trust in the strength of God to change hearts, not in the ability of the young man to do the changing.

HOW DO WE INITIATE?

Discipleship begins by bringing multiple generations of men together. For example, you could simply invite young men to your men's ministry events and be intentional about including them while they are there. Our ministry emphasizes outings, events, and trips that give plenty of time for shared experiences and conversations. Some of my lifelong friendships with younger men were launched *on the way* to events. Conversations happen naturally while traveling to sporting events, ministry sites, stadium rallies, remote churches, retreat centers, and campsites.

TREATING THEM LIKE FUTURE MEN

I once asked a thirteen-year-old boy why he chose to listen to me. He responded, "You don't talk to me like I'm a child." Young men, especially around puberty, want to be recognized as progressing from a boy to a man, a transition that is woefully foggy in our culture. You can gain the ear of a young man by challenging him, asking his opinion, and valuing his contributions. Set the bar reasonably high. See him where he will be, not where he is today.

USING THE WHOLE BODY
TO DISCIPLE THE WHOLE BOY

Ministry to young men is more than teaching them to memorize the Bible. We must also help them to be content with their bodies, recognize and respond to their emotions in a way that honors God, navigate the complexities of living with other people, and apply the truths of God's Word in practical ways.

When I was a young man, an older man named Rob taught me to love the Bible. But he was not the man to look to for help in relationships. Another man, Joe, taught me practical life skills that I use today, but he had trouble responding to difficulties with joy. One man may not be equipped to disciple in several different areas, and that's okay. The body of Christ is a diverse body for a reason.

MASCULINITY COMES IN MANY SHAPES AND SIZES

The diversity that God has designed into the fabric of his creation extends into the fabric of masculinity as well. Manhood has many healthy expressions. Those of us in ministry to young men must be careful not to communicate an unbiblical, narrow view of what it means to be a man. King David was a warrior, but he was also an artist, poet, musician, philosopher, reader, deep thinker, and dancer who could weep as openly and strongly as he was able to issue a battle cry.

One reason we struggle to reach the millennial heart is that we may be trying to squeeze men into masculine models *we* have drawn, not God. This can produce the responses we are trying to prevent: young men who don't fit the profile may run away from godly masculinity and into the arms of gender confusion and homosexuality. Guard your men against a caricature that accentuates only one aspect of masculinity.

DON'T TRIVIALIZE

Grown men tend to dismiss the concerns of young men. Your men must be reminded that Jesus doesn't trivialize *our* fears even though they are just as baseless from his perspective. Jesus understands our concerns and points us back to the truth and security of the gospel and the hope we have in the sovereign love of God. A young man will listen to an older man who takes his concerns seriously and then shows him how to view his fears through the lens of biblical truth.

AUTHENTICITY

Millennials can quickly pick out posers and pretenders. Therefore, it's vital to train your men to simply be who God has designed them to be. They should not pretend to be better or cooler than they are. This form of manipulation does not honor God, nor does it impress young men.

Tom was a short, stocky, balding middle-aged man who oversaw the discipleship ministry of my boyhood church. No one would have called Tom "cool." I certainly didn't. But what I saw every week was a man who sacrificed time to invest in the lives of young men like me. He encouraged me, corrected me, and showed interest in my life. He never sought to be anything but what God designed him to be. He earned my respect, and I listened to him.

FEAR AND SHAME

I'd been meeting with fourteen-year-old Sean almost every week for eighteen months. I thought I had earned his trust because he had opened up about some deep issues. We were talking about his struggles with the Internet. He claimed to be clean, but I'd seen his browsing history from the night before. I let him lie to me for a few minutes, then I revealed what I knew. His face went pale and his smile morphed into a look of shame. I quickly assured him that my love for him was in no way lessened by his fall and even by his deceit. Then I asked him why he lied to me. He was finally honest: he was afraid of disappointing me.

Young men share a strong desire to impress their mentors. Ironically, the more they get to know and trust us, the more they fear our disappointment and rejection. Make sure the young men you mentor know that your love for them cannot be earned, just as God's love cannot be earned.

SHARING OUR STORIES

One of the important ways to connect with young men is to tell your story. The millennial mind responds to authentic stories of struggle and victory in a particularly deep way. When a young man understands that you have also struggled, you wash away his fear and prepare his heart for what you have to say.

Remember what it was like to be a young man? You experienced the same turbulence in your head, your heart, and between your legs. But a young man doesn't naturally see this. You're old—he's young. He often thinks you can't possibly understand what he's feeling.

I'd spent two years teaching a young man named Paul. One day, I shared in a brief text, admitting my own struggle with sexual sin. He replied, "Thank you for that text. Honestly, probably my favorite thing you have sent me." Teach your mentors to humbly and appropriately share their stories. They are often far more effective than our lectures.

DON'T REPLACE DAD

Our society is suffering an epidemic of fatherlessness. As Christian mentors, we must be careful not to make things worse by unintentionally supplanting a young man's father. Boys need their dads, and dads need their boys.

Contrary to popular opinion, young men *do* care about the voice of the older generation. They want the attention and care of their fathers and other mature men. Let this inspire your men as they minister to the men of tomorrow.

28

DISCIPLING MEN IN THE MARKETPLACE

(BAX KEGANS)

Bax Kegans is a Christian husband, father, salesman, and men's leader from Baton Rouge, Louisiana. He currently serves at Parkview Baptist Church (pbcbr.org) and with Gulf South Men (gulfsouthmen.org).

Jesus grew up in a working-class household in Nazareth. Joseph and Mary were faithful followers of God, making sure Jesus and his siblings were in the temple each week, making yearly trips to Jerusalem. Joseph was a carpenter; Jesus grew up learning the trade (see Mark 6:3). I imagine Joseph and Jesus came into contact with some rough characters. In the same way, we encounter all sorts of colorful people in our day-to-day lives on the job.

It's worth remembering that when Jesus began recruiting disciples, he didn't head to Jerusalem and recruit the top students out of the temple. Rather, he went to the marketplace. He found his initial core group at work, convincing them to leave their fishing nets. He recruited Matthew away from his tax booth. These were not theological scholars; they were working-class guys.

GETTING OFF THE FENCE

If you truly desire to disciple men in the marketplace, you must get off the fence and fully surrender to the lordship of Jesus. To effectively share Christ, a man must "deny himself, and take up his cross, and follow Me" (Matthew 16:24 NKJV).

From 1994 to 2001, I lived a compartmentalized life as a Christian and an outside salesman. It wasn't until a retired chemical engineer engaged me at church and invited me to breakfast with other young men—another salesman, a small-business owner, two accountants from an industrial engineering firm, an IT professional, and a truck driver—that I was encouraged to be a Christian salesman.

Off the fence and following Jesus, I became more intentional in reading and studying God's Word daily and connecting with other believers during the week. That included small groups with men from church and the marketplace. A commitment to these groups and an accountability partner helped me overcome the sins I kept falling into.

EQUIP YOUR MEN TO MINISTER TO MEN IN THE MARKETPLACE

As a pastor or leader in a local church, your role is to awaken the men of your church to be more intentional about identifying as followers of Christ seven days a week. Brian Doyle of Iron Sharpens Iron encourages pastors to call the men down at the end of Sunday worship and challenge them to be bold and intentional about their faith. A savvy senior pastor might be convinced to do a short sermon series specifically targeted at men, even though statistically they make up less than half of your adult members. As a leader of men, you have the responsibility to challenge men to see their jobsites as fields ripe for the harvest.

ALREADY IN THE MARKETPLACE?

As individuals and as a group, routinely ask God to reveal opportunities to connect with other men who need to hear the gospel. Pray also for courage, humility, and the right words to speak. On the job, look for opportunities to talk about "how God is working in my life." Monday morning in the breakroom, or when the vending truck rolls up, it's okay to mention something you "heard at church on Sunday." Talk about how excited you are about a men's retreat, special speaker at your church, or upcoming mission trip. Invite guys to join you.

Get over being worried about what other people in the office think. You are a child of God, a fisher of men. Don't hide your Bible reading during lunch; invite someone to join you and discuss what you're reading. When conversations about movies come up, feel free to chime in with a review of the latest movie with a Christian theme. Make your faith a part of your work life.

At one of your large men's gatherings, teach on this concept and invite some guys up front to do some role playing. Keep it light. Take fear out of the equation. Men shouldn't hide their relationship with Christ. Remember, approved workmen are not ashamed (see 2 Timothy 2:15).

Get comfortable with some open-ended questions that might spark a dialogue with a coworker. "How are your kids? It's a challenge balancing work and home, isn't it? How was your weekend? Seen any decent movies recently?" After gathering some personal insight on your new friend, go deeper. "Do you ever think about spiritual things? Did you go to church when you were a kid? What's the biggest thing in your life right now?" Or even, "Can I tell you what keeps me going when life gets hard?" Of course, it's not an interrogation. It's a dialogue between two work colleagues, neither of which have all the answers.

Still, if a man is recognized as a Christian on the job, he should not be surprised when a colleague with a crisis comes to him for advice. After all, a man who lives his faith might have answers not found in today's spiritually void culture. In that case, I encourage you to listen and then offer to pray with them about the situation. In fifteen years, I've only had one person refuse an offer of prayer. If the colleague doesn't have a Bible, then get him one; begin to search God's Word for guidance and direction to walk him through the crisis. Share the gospel and invite him to join you for worship at your church if he's not already connected.

In a strange twist of fate, work colleagues who seem the furthest from God might be the ones who are most likely to respond to your outreach. That guy who's angry, broke, or recently divorced needs a friend. And he can find that friend in Jesus.

GETTING MARKETPLACE MEN TOGETHER

Encourage the men in your ministry to join or start a Bible study or small group among coworkers or industry partners. You may be surprised at how many companies allow employees to use a meeting room for opening their Bibles once a week over lunch or before work. Be sure to respect your host by cleaning up and not going past the allotted time. Local coffee shops and restaurants are honored and eager to have men gather in their back room or a corner of their shops once a week. Just remember to tip well.

As a men's leader, begin to track these groups. Keep a record of times and places where Christian men are meeting. Make sure each group is welcoming to new attendees. When any man begins to make a connection with a seeker, he should be able to say something like, "I meet every Thursday over lunch with a group of guys to talk about being better husbands and fathers, and share how God is working in our lives. You are more than welcome to check it out."

In every shop, office, factory, and institution, men are struggling with their marriages, parenting, finances, and so on. Isn't it our responsibility to connect them to disciples they can relate with? You're not alone. Resources are available. CBMC (Christian Business Men's Connection, cbmc.com) has local teams throughout the US and ninety-five other countries. The Iron Sharpens Iron Conference Network works alongside a network of regional men's ministries (ironsharpensiron .net). Ask around and you'll find industry-specific groups, including Oilfield Christian Fellowship or Lawyers' Christian Fellowship. Also, make time for regional conferences or retreats that emphasize workplace ministry.

Jesus ministered in the marketplace. He was a faithful follower of his Father God as a carpenter. He began his public ministry in the marketplace, calling out seven fishermen, a tax collector, and four tradesmen. He didn't say, "When you are ready and get your affairs in order, I'll be waiting for you." Mark 8 describes how Jesus called them to immediately take up their cross and follow him. And that they did.

29

REACHING THE NEXT GENERATION OF MEN

(DR. CHUCK STECKER)

Chuck Stecker is the president and founder of A Chosen Generation, which helps churches and families create strategies for intergenerational ministry. Chuck is an ordained minister, served in the military for twenty-three years, and is the author of *Men of Honor Women of Virtue: The Power of Rites of Passage into Godly Adulthood.* Find out more at achosengeneration.info.

I t seems like everyone in ministry is asking, "How do we reach the next generation?" Some believe the sky is falling and if we do not work hard to accommodate and win the younger generation, the local church is going to die and Christianity will fade into a once-followed religion of the past. News flash: God wins and his church will prevail.

That said, there are significant reasons to connect with the younger generation of men and create clear paths for them to develop a personal faith of their own and become the world changers God created them to be. First, let's consider the reasons so many of us oldsters find it difficult to reach the next generation of young men:

- We tend to judge others by their actions, while we judge ourselves by our intentions.

- We believe they'll grow up and mature on their own.
- We are not that comfortable around them; perhaps, in time, they will be more like us.
- We built this church, and frankly, we are not ready to change the music and structure just to accommodate a generation that has not yet proven themselves.

Despite our excuses, we can't deny the biblical command to reach the next generation and prepare them for works greater than what we have done. Throughout Scripture, we see the phrase "generation to generation." Psalm 145:4 tells us, "One generation shall commend your works to another, and shall declare your mighty acts" (ESV). We should never forget that we were once the younger generation. Years ago, someone saw a value in us we may not have seen in ourselves, and they gave us a chance to become who we are today.

You must admit the *why* of this topic is much easier than the *how*. Although your gut—and maybe the Holy Spirit—tells you that the answer to the *how* question begins with you: the men's ministry leader or pastor. Young men respond to men who are sincere, intentional, available, trustworthy, and can be respected. The current generation of younger men are not "snowflakes," as the press has sometimes depicted them. They are young men who truly want to make a difference and want to be around men who will believe in them.

In their book *Lost and Found*, Ed Stetzer, Richie Stanley, and Jason Hayes identify four markers or characteristics of churches reaching the next generation:

- Community
- Depth (and content)
- Responsibility
- Cross-generational connection

Authentic community is a critical desire of most young men. In this generation, far too many men are involved in social-media communities—Facebook, Instagram, and Snapchat—that have no shared values or accountability. Group activities such as biking, skiing, or going to sporting events may seem like communities, but they often lack the key ingredients of mutual trust, allegiance, and the assurance of believing in each other.

The coming generation also craves *depth and content*. Unfortunately, there is an underlying feeling that we, as the older generation, do not trust them with anything too difficult. Paraphrasing the apostle Paul, they feel we are trying to feed them milk while they want meat.

Responsibility should be translated into leadership opportunities. While speaking to older men, I have asked the question, "How many of you have invested in or raised up a young man in leadership that you would be willing to serve under?" Too many of us older guys want to raise up leaders to lead anyone but us. Simply put, if you want to reach men of all generations, ethnic backgrounds, and economic levels, and your leadership is a bunch of older "white men," you are most likely not going to be successful over the long haul.

Finally, there needs to be opportunities for *cross-generational connections*. Actually, I prefer the term "intergenerational relationships." Young men are hungry for older men who will invest and believe in, mentor, coach, and encourage them.

If you are truly committed to reaching, equipping, training, empowering, and releasing the next generation of men for God's glory, there are three key concepts that must not be overlooked: (1) men must be invited by another man they respect and trust; (2) men must be invited by another man they respect and trust; and (3) men must be invited by another man they respect and trust. To summarize for clarity: men must be invited by another man they respect and trust.

Several years ago, my good friend Jim Ladd, senior pastor at Evergreen Christian Community Church, developed and taught me a concept simply stated as "in such a way as." By identifying a goal, such as gaining the respect and trust of younger men, we can approach every ministry, outreach, or event with a new purpose. How do we do a Saturday breakfast in such a way as to gain the respect of younger men? How do we recruit for missions in such a way as to gain the trust of younger men? How do we love our wives in such a way as to gain the respect and trust of younger men? We may have more success when we stop trying to minister *to* men and focus instead on ministering *through* men. For sure, young men do not want to be considered a statistic or someone being recruited to bring down the average age of the men's ministry.

Another common mistake is to recruit the next generation by trying to act, talk, or dress like them. Acknowledge the vibrant energy and potential of youth, but please act your own age. That doesn't mean we should be boring. The Christian life is an adventure. Ministry to men should be a series of daring adventures launched from a firm foundation. Gone are the days, if they ever existed, when men could be invited to a small group where they would be expected to "share." The word *share* is enough to make any man puke. However, sharing does happen organically in the course of an activity. John Eldredge wrote:

> The beauty of a chairlift—or a car, fishing boat, duck blind, woodshop table—is that you aren't facing each other the whole time, in a forced and awkward intimacy. It allows a young man the kind of room he needs for deep conversations to come out, the "focus" set on something else. It's far better, far truer to the masculine soul than sitting around in the church basement or a Sunday school room in a circle of chairs, looking at one another, and being told to "share." If you want to get a boy or a man talking, get him out doing something.[1]

One win-win strategy to engage men of different generations is to get them serving someone else, together. New Commandment Ministries (newcommandment.org) equips men to meet the tangible needs of widows, single moms, and the disabled. Men of all ages can serve together in a proven structure that meets incredible needs.

Younger men really are seeking older role models. But they don't want to be overwhelmed by anyone's personal agenda. Whether you call it coaching or mentoring, the goal is to come alongside and offer encouragement. Some define mentoring as *putting in*, while coaching is pulling out. Others teach that coaching does not give direction, but only asks questions. In any case, we must be careful not to define ourselves out of effectiveness.

My experience with young men is that they need someone who is available, nonjudgmental, encouraging, and willing to invest his experience. I call that person an "EnCoMentor" (an encourager, coach, and mentor). I meet weekly with men of all ages. Some days they need me to listen and encourage, while on other days, they are seeking advice. Yet other meetings reveal the need for me to introduce them to someone who is more qualified than I am on a specific subject. As an EnCoMentor, I encourage, coach, and mentor, depending on the need at the time.

Finally, to reach the next generation of men, we must teach older men to be available. A valuable phrase, one you probably already use, is, "How about a cup of coffee this week?" I have found that phrase works, even if he or you don't drink coffee.

Your words, tone, and body language all send out signals as to whether you are available. But don't make it more complicated than it is. Establish an open-door policy at your office, be self-deprecating, admit your own spiritual missteps, and acknowledge there are differences between the generations. These things make you accessible and available. And in case you missed it earlier, here's the key to reaching the next generation of men: they must be invited by another man they respect and trust.

Men of all ages want to make a difference. Men of all ages want to be around men who will mentor, coach, and encourage them. Lastly, men of all ages are looking for older men who are available. Perhaps you're that man!

RECOMMENDED READING

- Jim Grassi, *Building a Ministry of Spiritual Mentoring* (Nashville, TN: Thomas Nelson, 2014).
- Ken Ham, with Jeff Kinley, *Ready to Return* (Green Forest, AR: Master Books, 2015).
- Brad Lomenick, *The Catalyst Leader: 8 Essentials for Becoming a Change Maker* (Nashville, TN: Thomas Nelson, 2013).
- Andy Stanley, *Deep and Wide: Creating Churches Unchurched People Love to Attend* (Grand Rapids, MI: Zondervan, 2012).

- Andy Stanley, *Next Generation Leader: Five Essentials for Those Who Will Shape the Future* (Portland, OR: Multnomah Books, 2006).
- Ed Stetzer, Ritchie Stanley, and Jason Hayes, *Lost and Found: The Younger Unchurched and the Churches That Reach Them* (Nashville, TN: B&H Publishing, 2009).

Section VI

PRAYER, TEACHING, AND EVANGELISM

30

TEACHING FOR
THE MALE BRAIN

(DAVID MURROW)

David Murrow is the best-selling author of *Why Men Hate Going to Church* and several other books. He is the founder of Church for Men, an organization that helps congregations reach more men and boys. His website is ChurchForMen.com.

I t takes twenty hours to prepare a message and twenty minutes for men to forget it.

Think back to the last church service you attended. Somebody preached a sermon, right? Do you remember the topic? Can you recall even one sentence the pastor said? How about the last men's meeting you attended? Was there a speaker? What was his topic? What Bible verses did he quote?

God's Word is preached, presented, and taught hundreds of thousands of times each week, but why isn't it having a greater impact? It is because men are forgetting what they hear just moments after they hear it. The Word is being sown, but it is failing to implant and grow in the hearts of the men who hear it (see Matthew 13:4).

It would be easy to pin this failure on poor preaching or men's stony hearts. But in many cases, the fault lies not with the messenger, the message, or the men—the problem is in the *method*.

Most Christian teaching is delivered verbally. Somebody stands up and talks. People listen. Mission accomplished, right?

Not really. The verbal regions of a man's brain are typically smaller

157

and less interconnected than those in a woman's brain. The typical man is less able to process a stream of verbal content, such as a lecture or a sermon. However, the male brain is good at recalling and manipulating three-dimensional objects moving through space. So if you want to teach for the male brain, you must tie your words to common 3-D objects men see all the time.

Jesus knew this. He built his teaching around things his hearers saw every day. Christ used sheep, wheat, coins, cadavers, lakes, fig trees, loaves, fish, children, nets, blind men, and many other physical objects to convey spiritual truths. As a result, his teachings are still with us today. Why? *Because men remembered them.* Men recalled them so vividly they could write them down years after they happened.

If we are serious about implanting God's Word in men's hearts, we must do what Jesus did—use live, object-based illustrations when we teach men (OBIs).

THE METHOD

You may be thinking, *I'm not creative enough to come up with an OBI.* Baloney. Any Christian can create a memorable object-based illustration. I've created dozens of them, and I'm not even a preacher. Let me walk you through the process. Along the way, I'll give you an example you're free to steal.

First, pray and ask God for the gift of creativity. God is first and foremost a Creator, and you're made in his image (Genesis 1:1). Ask him to give you the gift of a creative OBI so people will remember his Word.

Second, identify the central point you're trying to convey. What's the most important thing you want men to take away from your teaching? Let's say your topic is salvation by faith versus works, and your key verse is Ephesians 2:8–9: "For by grace you have been saved through faith. And this is not your own doing; it is the gift of God, not a result of works, so that no one may boast" (ESV).

Third, ask, what's an object that's *like* my central point? What's analogous to a free gift? Thinking … thinking … eureka! Salvation is like getting a gift card for your birthday. Somebody else paid the price; you get the benefit.

Fourth, develop the idea even further. Are there any other closely related objects that fit your analogy? Thinking … thinking … yes! Salvation is *not* like a debit card, where you deposit your own good works into the account, hoping to withdraw them later. Salvation is *not* like a credit card where you work to pay back your crushing debt to God.

Now, build your entire message around this one metaphor. Here's a rough outline of how I'd present this: Hold up a debit card and explain how you deposit your money into the bank and withdraw it when you need it. The application is that there are many debit-card religions out there. Liken a debit card to karma, the religious concept that you must do good to receive good. Then hold up a credit card and explain how the bank lends you money that you must repay with interest. Liken the credit card to legalistic religions where the individual pays his or her own debt to God through religious fervor. Last of all, hold up a gift card. Explain that you did nothing to deserve this card; someone else paid for it and gave it freely to you. Liken the gift card to Christianity. Jesus paid for the card; your only responsibility is to receive it.

From this point, you can go in many different directions. Give an invitation to receive God's gift of salvation; challenge the spiritualists and legalists in the congregation to give up on debit-card and credit-card religions; then finish the message by handing the gift card to someone who could really use it.

Before you try this, here are four important tips to remember:

1. Before you teach, rehearse! Practice your OBI in front of the mirror or with a friend. Have it down pat before you speak.
2. It's better to stick with one OBI per message, rather than having multiple illustrations. Remember the saying: don't mix your metaphors. Men will retain one strong OBI more readily than three or four weak ones.
3. You may be tempted to set up your talk with a two-minute OBI, then spend the rest of your time delivering a traditional sermon. That's a mistake. If you really want your point to stick in men's minds, build your entire talk around your metaphor. Come back to it again and again. For example, keep holding those credit cards up as you make your points.

4. Coin a phrase or phrases to reinforce the message. For example, "Debit-Card Religion" and "Gift-Card Faith." Use your phrases repeatedly as you teach. In time, your people will begin using these phrases to exhort one another.

THE DOWNSIDES

About 90 percent of your hearers will really appreciate this technique; the other 10 percent will hate it. They will say things like:

- "This is juvenile. If I want a kids' lesson, I'll go to Sunday school."
- "Object lessons are a gimmick. They're a crutch for the spiritually immature."
- "This is milk. Give me the pure meat of God's Word, preached with power!"

How do we answer our critics? Agree with them. Tell them you're simplifying the message to reach the immature and the unchurched (implying that your critics, of course, are spiritual giants). And then gently remind them of how frequently Jesus used OBIs in his ministry.

THE FRUIT

You may be thinking, *Wow, I'd love to use more OBIs, but it seems like a lot of extra work.* But it's really not. A good OBI can actually save you time in preparation. And the benefits are huge:

1. *Greater retention.* Men will think about the illustration all week long. And some men will remember the point of your message weeks, months, or even years later.
2. *Life situations will remind men of what they learned.* For example, every time your men see a debit, credit, or gift card, they will recall God's free gift of salvation.
3. *You'll see more men in your church.* If your pastor brings an OBI into the pulpit every week, I guarantee that your church will grow. And men will be leading the parade.
4. *Greater interest among the men.* The male brain is also wired for novelty. Men love to be surprised. They'll anticipate each message, wondering, *What's he going to do this week?*

5. *Men will be emboldened to invite their friends to church.* Interesting sermons encourage people to invite their friends. And visitors generally love OBIs because they help them understand complex spiritual truths.

6. *People will start using the illustrations to disciple one another.* It's true. I've seen it happen. Guys will get their wallets out and share their faith using their credit, debit, and gift cards. And guys will use the metaphor to challenge each other: "Hey, knock it off! You're practicing debit-card Christianity, dude!"

7. *Men are equipped to disciple their children.* Fathers who would never re-preach a sermon will eagerly reenact an OBI with their kids at home.

8. *Viral sharing.* Not long ago, a three-minute video clip showed up in my Facebook feed featuring a pastor clutching a balance beam for dear life (Google search: pastor balance beam). He was illustrating how timid most Christians are. The clip has been viewed almost 1.5 million times and has been copied by pastors around the globe.

Finally, let me address the elephant in the room: If we teach for the male brain, will females feel left out? Not at all. Women benefit from OBIs just as much as men. Our children are growing up in a visual culture. Television, the Internet, and social media—they are all about images. Innovative companies, schools, and universities are moving away from lectures and bullet points toward interactive lessons involving 3-D objects.

Is this really something new? Christ taught men this way two thousand years ago, and those men turned the world upside down. We may not be able to walk on water, heal a paralytic, or wither a fig tree, but with God's help we can take common, everyday objects and create unforgettable illustrations that change men's lives.

31

GOD'S MEN PRAY

(EDWARD BARTLE)

Reverend Edward (Ed) Bartle, who is the associate rector at St. George Episcopal Church, The Villages, Florida, was ordained to the priesthood after a career in criminal justice and teaching. Contact Ed at ebbartle@aol.com.

Why are men uncomfortable praying? What stands in their way to communicate with God? One of my male parishioners answered my question in one word: *humility*. We must overcome the macho-man image, the I-am-a-rock image, and understand that we are made in God's image for a purpose. We need to understand we don't need to try to be more spiritual; we don't need a degree in theology to pray.

I grew up in a generation that expected men to be the self-sufficient and self-reliant protector guaranteeing safety for our families. Neediness is for sissies. So it stands to reason that a man who won't even stop to ask for directions probably won't go to a "higher authority" for help.

Before entering seminary, I spent forty years in criminal justice as a law-enforcement officer, a private investigator, and a college instructor in the field. During those years, I witnessed every form of good and evil that humans can inflict upon one another. I saw anger and hate toward others and toward God. And I saw miracles take place, with joyful prayer of thanksgiving to God.

One event from more than thirty years ago haunts my memory

and mocks the idea that a man is the ultimate protector of his family. I was working an insurance investigation on a traffic fatality case involving the death of a mother and daughter. During the interview, the husband revealed the details of the accident: a teenage girl stole a relative's car and took it for a joyride. As he and his family were driving through a community, the girl in the stolen car came off a hill at a high rate of speed and struck the family car broadside, killing the mother and the daughter. With tears in his eyes, he looked me in the face and said, "I always thought I could protect my family, and within seconds I lost them—there was nothing I could do."

There was a time in my life when I was in serious despair. My life was unraveling, and there seemed no way out of the depression. I found myself sitting in the churchyard near the memorial garden where my mother had been interred. With tears in my eyes, I asked the proverbial question, "Why, God?" Our parish priest found me there and comforted me. As the years went by, he became a strong mentor and friend. Eventually he was called to be the rector at a different parish. Again, I asked, "Why, God? Who can I now turn to for guidance and strength?" The answer was immediate: *How about me?*

My father was an ordained deacon in the Episcopal Church and lovingly served God and his parish for almost forty years. When he retired, he was bestowed the title Deacon Emeritus. In many ways, he was my higher authority. Not taking anything away from my love for our God and Savior, I knew I could always call upon my earthly father in times of need. I rarely needed assistance from him, probably because I thought I could "do all things" myself, but it was comforting to know Dad was there when I needed him. A few years ago, he went to heaven. Again, I was left thinking, *Who can I turn to now?* God once again demonstrated his love and patience through his clear response, *Try me! I'm here when you need me.*

In his book *Pastoring Men*, Patrick Morley defines prayer like this:

> Prayer is God's designated means of pouring our hearts out to Him, of personal relationship, of communion, of praising and worshiping Him, of getting our needs met or interceding for others, of ushering the kingdom of God into human affairs.

Prayer is our means to seek and receive forgiveness, pledge allegiance to Jesus, express gratitude for his "Goodness and unfailing love that will pursue me all the days of my life" (Psalm 23:6 NLT). Prayer is the means of healing, of mercy, of grace, of wisdom and guidance, and of filling by the Holy Spirit.[1]

How do we go about learning to pray? It's not really that complicated. As children, we learned to talk so that we could communicate with others. If we were hungry, we learned to ask to be fed. When we were ill, we learned to ask to be cared for. When we received, we learned to say thank you. When we were lost, we learned to seek direction. And so, I can almost imagine God using the vernacular expression "Duh!"

He might also say, *Talk to me. I already know what's on your heart and mind, but I want to hear you say it. Do you not recall my Son, Jesus, in the gospel of Luke being asked by his disciples how to pray?* Recall how Jesus spelled it out for them: "When you pray, say: 'Father, hallowed be your name, your kingdom come. Give us each day our daily bread. Forgive us our sins, for we also forgive everyone who sins against us, and lead us not into temptation'" (Luke 11:2–4). In Matthew, he gives further instructions:

> "And when you pray, do not be like the hypocrites, for they love to pray standing in the synagogues and on the street corners to be seen by others. Truly I tell you, they have received their reward in full. But when you pray, go into your room, close the door and pray to your Father, who is unseen. Then your Father, who sees what is done in secret, will reward you. And when you pray, do not keep on babbling like pagans, for they think they will be heard because of their many words. Do not be like them, for your Father knows what you need before you ask him." (Matthew 6:5–8)

Pastor and author John Ortberg said, "If you believe in God, you have already begun to pray—to enter into a dialogue with him—because believing in God means believing he is always present, always listening to what you say. To come to believe is to begin to pray, because of the constancy of God's presence."[2]

Consciously or subconsciously, we pray almost continuously. "Oh my God" is such a common phrase used today. We hear the words used when someone receives a great gift or is surprised by an event, such as winning the lottery. We hear the words when someone is in disbelief, as with a death or serious accident involving a loved one. In many cases, it's used thoughtlessly—perhaps even recklessly—especially on reality television shows. You've likely seen a home-improvement show during which a couple exclaims that phrase as they enter each newly decorated room. Wouldn't they be surprised if God's voice boomed out, "Yes, my children? I'm here for you."

The phrase really is the beginning of what should be a prayer. God is waiting for the rest of the prayer that never comes. As those who believe in and trust God, perhaps we should allow the expression "Oh my God" to remind us to complete our own thoughts, prayers, and thanksgivings to him. Ortberg again tells us, "The goal of prayer is to live all of my life and speak all of my words in the joyful awareness of the presence of God."[3]

In his book *Prayer: Finding the Heart's True Home*, Richard J. Foster writes:

In the beginning we are indeed the subject and center of our prayers. But in God's time and in God's way a Copernican revolution takes place in our heart. Slowly, almost imperceptibly, there is a shift in our center of gravity. We pass from thinking of God as part of our life to the realization that we are part of his life.[4]

Foster goes on to offer a simple prayer:

Dear Jesus, how desperately I need to learn to pray. And yet when I am honest, I know that I often do not even want to pray. I am distracted!
I am stubborn!
I am self-centered!
In your mercy, Jesus, bring my "want-er" more in line with my "need-er" so that I can come to want what I need.
In your name and for your sake, I pray. —Amen.[5]

And finally, when all else fails, there is always the Jesus Prayer: "Lord Jesus, Son of the Father, have mercy on me, a sinner!"

Dear brothers, take this to heart and invite every man you know to do the same. Regularly, daily, unceasingly, talk with our Father as you would with your best friend, for he is the best friend you will ever have.

32

THE POWER OF MEN PRAYING TOGETHER

(K. C. DICKIE)

K. C. Dickie is the founder and director of the Men's Equipping Network, which prayerfully connects, equips, and challenges men to serve the community. For more information or to join the Mighty Men Movement, visit mensequippingnetwork.com.

I n the spring of 2000, two men began to pray together at their church in Fresno, California, with the desire to bless their pastor, their church, their community, and their families. They had no idea what it would lead to. They met weekly at five each Friday morning, and because of the joy they had in doing so, they began to invite others to join them. Two turned into five, five into ten, and so on. That group today, fifteen years later, has as many as fifty men gathering to pray together on a weekly basis. In fact, that group has never missed a Friday in those fifteen years.

Those two men were myself and a close friend, Brian Cochran. Today, twenty-five men's prayer groups meet across our city for the same purpose that started in the beginning—to bless families, pastors, churches, and our communities.

Hebrews 10:24–25 tell us, "And let us consider how to stir up one another to love and good works, not neglecting to meet together, as is the habit of some, but encouraging one another, and all the more as you see the Day drawing near" (ESV). This is precisely what happens as men join as a band of brothers in these prayer groups. In fact, I'll go as far as to say that these men's groups epitomize what men's ministry is all about. Some of these groups have been meeting for fourteen years, some for ten, and others for eight. The reason these groups flourish is that men are encouraged when they meet. They receive prayer, there is that great bonding that takes place, and they learn how to pray by listening to others pray.

But here is the most important aspect of men praying together: They are developing *intimacy with Christ*. This is a game changer. I'll go out on a limb and say that until a man finds intimacy with Christ, he'll remain lukewarm in his relationship with God.

Through God's Word, we receive the mind of Christ; through prayer, we receive the very heart of Christ. Where the two intersect, when a man spends time in the Word and time in prayer, that's the sweet spot for a man to be. Unfortunately, prayer, as powerful as it is, is the most underutilized arrow in the Christian quiver and in the church today.

I've had a front-row seat for sixteen years, watching men who have never really spent any real time in prayer, learning how to pray. It's like watching an infant crawl, walk, and then run. Little by little, they begin to open up and find intimacy with God; men who have never served have now become deacons and ushers in the church. I've had wives thank me for getting their husbands involved in our group because they tell me *it has changed them.*

Three years ago, God gave me a vision of ten thousand men partnering with us in prayer. The goal of the Mighty Men Movement is to build an army of the Lord, right here in Fresno. Our breakfasts have a "special forces" theme and focus on three things: to grow men's monthly prayer groups; to motivate men to take active roles in their churches and families; and to grab hold of inviting "just one more" to the following month's breakfast. These breakfasts are held on Thursday mornings from six to seven thirty, so as not to take up weekends.

Those monthly outreach events have significantly increased the number of men who are actively involved in weekly prayer groups. These hour-long gatherings led by a facilitator typically meet in the morning at church before guys head off to start their day. We call them "breakfasts," but it's not about food for our bodies. Coffee is a must, but you don't have to get fancy with any other sweets or treats. These are guys who have come to pray. Numbers vary, but our weekly gathering often includes forty or more men.

We sit in a circle facing each other and begin by not asking anything of God, but just seeking his face in worship and praise. We ask a few men to individually lead, and an intimacy with God begins almost immediately. We then go to our knees for a few minutes in silent confession. The goal is for every man to leave nothing unconfessed, nothing to impede our prayers, so we're able to come before God with clean hands and pure hearts. There's great humility in kneeling before an almighty God.

That leads naturally to a worship song with everybody standing, some with arms outstretched, some with heads raised to the heavens. It's an awesome time! Then one of the men, who was assigned the previous week, gives a ten-minute devotional. This is followed by intercessory prayer, which includes praying for the church, our communities, and our families. We pray up and out, not up and in. Lastly, we break into groups of three so that each man gets to pray for others and receive prayer. At the end, someone closes us in prayer.

This is the basic format, but we always leave room for the Holy Spirit to move. Often some issue arises and we'll stop, bring a person into the center of the room, lay hands on him, and pray about that particular issue.

Throughout the hour, we try to be sensitive to the specific needs of the men, especially newcomers. We let men know that if they aren't comfortable praying out loud, that's okay. We also let them know to be brief in their prayers so others will have a chance to pray too.

It's worth noting that these prayer groups are different than small groups and Bible studies that one may be more familiar with. Most of the attendees get solid teaching in other venues during the week. We're giving men an opportunity to do something that doesn't happen enough in our busy lives—to come humbly, honestly, and regularly before God's throne.

And it's working. Each of these groups is growing because men are finding personal benefit and inviting others to do the same. We use the concept of "Lord, give me just one more" to grow the groups. We also invite the leadership teams from other local churches to join us for our monthly and weekly events. When a newcomer, even an experienced pastor, sees what happens when men pray, he is eager to incorporate this strategy in his own church.

James 5:16 holds an amazing promise for us: "The effectual fervent prayer of a righteous man availeth much" (KJV). If the prayer of one man avails much, what might that equate to if ten thousand righteous men are united in prayer? Might that have the power to transform families, churches, communities, states, and even a nation? Might it even usher in revival?

Whether you're a pastor or a lay person, a rich man or a poor man, an educated man or uneducated, start to build a culture of prayer in your personal life and in the life of your church. You'll be amazed at the results. But really, you shouldn't be. The impact will be exactly as God promised.

33

DISPLACED DISCIPLESHIP

(SCOTT CAESAR)

Scott Caesar is the founder and men's pastor of the Men's Discipleship Network. He is the author of the W.E.A.P.O.N.S. Curriculum® used throughout churches today. His passion is to assist in systematizing male discipleship for the local church. Scott's website is mensdiscipleshipnetwork.com.

It was Sunday lunch—the end of a men's retreat made in heaven. Smiles, bro hugs, high fives, and faces that reflected God's love. One man approached me, overflowing with excitement. He had found freedom in God's love through the Spirit of sonship. His life was changed that weekend, but he had almost chosen not to come. "I did not want to get the usual men's dressing down," he whispered. "You know, the man of responsibility and accountability deal. Thank you for making me drop my guns."

Men's ministry has gained a reputation as a hammer-the-men time. In churches across America, the gospel of grace has been displaced by a gospel of good, which defines biblical manhood as a quest not for freedom in Christ, but for virtues and moral purity. Somehow, we have pushed aside the cross and have begun to think we can meet God's standards of goodness by heaping on guilt, working harder, and saving ourselves.

That conflicts with what the apostle Paul writes in Ephesians 2:8: "For it is by grace you have been saved, through faith—and this is not from yourselves, it is the gift of God." Moral effort must never take the place of grace. The signs of displacement are often seen in the families of men we disciple. When a man is out of place, his wife is *misplaced*, his children are *displaced*, and God is *replaced*.

There's no denying that men who truly follow Jesus will live lives of honor. Integrity, servanthood, faithful fathering, and loving our wives as Christ loved the church are benchmarks for every Christian man. But when a man takes a *good* thing and makes it a *God* thing, it becomes a *bad* thing. If a spirit of legalism has crept into the men we serve, should we not engage this cultural stronghold when teaching our men?

I often start Men's Discipleship Network events with this question: "How many of you today have a goal to become a better Christian?" As hands go up, I say, "I have some good news for you and some bad news. The bad news is that it is not going to happen. You're as good as you are going to get as a son of God. The good news is the same: you're as good as you are going to get as a son of God. Yes, habits will change, wisdom will increase, enjoyment in Christ will abound, and you will mature, but no matter what you failed to do today or what you may have said or thought yesterday, God's acceptance and love for you at the cross is perfect, unconditional, and never ending." Romans 8:39 confirms that "neither height nor depth, nor anything else in all creation, will be able to separate us from the love of God that is in Christ Jesus our Lord."

We recently celebrated the twentieth anniversary of Men's Discipleship Network. After two decades, I realize my outreach to men could have been more effective had I not displaced the gospel of grace with the "gospel of good." I was a self-proclaimed moralist positioning the virtues of Christian manhood as a prize to be won instead of a fruit of obedience to a Savior and his amazing love. As a recovering performance addict, I am now fully persuaded that moralism (which is an emphasis on behavior) frustrates rather than frees a man.

All discipleship must start with the cross and its essential power. We must proclaim that moral muscle will not win the good fight. Only almighty God's forgiveness and love can demolish the burdens of self-hatred, condemnation, guilt, and shame. It melts away a man's insecurity and inadequacies while overwhelming his intellect with such acceptance that he is left with a desire to obey.

Obedience follows God's grace, which gives us power to say no. Paul wrote, "For the grace of God has appeared that offers salvation to all people. It teaches us to say 'No' to ungodliness and worldly passions, and to live self-controlled, upright and godly lives in this present age" (Titus 2:11–12). Let's explore three reasons so many Christian men are not maturing and growing in the faith.

REASON #1:
MEN EXHAUST THE ARM OF THEIR FLESH

Unfortunately, a common way to deal with lukewarmness among men today is to make them feel guilty and condemned. Guilt becomes the tool and motivator for guys to "act like men." A voice buried within whispers, "God is holy. You are not. Try harder."

This can appear to be effective—for a while—until a man exhausts his arm of flesh through Spirit-less effort. Soon, he starts to believe that maybe he is not good enough. He enters the Romans 7 maze that bemoans, "I should be a better husband and father, but I can't seem to be. I want to be a man of integrity, responsibility, and accountability, but I can't!" Discouragement follows. He will not mature without the Father's unconditional love that invites him to *get God before he gets good, not get good before he gets God!*

Effective discipleship must always include a man's identity. This is ushered in by the training of his mind and the clear understanding of his adoption as a son of God. Romans 8:6 says, "For the mind set on the flesh is death, but the mind set on the Spirit is life and peace" (NASB). And Galatians 4:7 promises, "Therefore you are no longer a slave but a son, and if a son, then an heir of God through Christ" (NKJV).

REASON# 2: CALLING MEN TO ACCOUNTABILITY BEFORE ACCEPTABILITY, RELATABILITY, AND SUSTAINABILITY IN GODLY RELATIONSHIPS

The most misused word in ministry to men today is *accountability*. A close second cousin is *admonish*. These wonderful biblical concepts, when used *out of context*, give counterfeit power to the legalist.

Jesus was a magnet to men. Likewise, men should be drawn to us too. There should be an expected spirit of freedom every time a man draws near to Christ, not a spirit of control that makes him want to hide. In a culture of honor, he sees Christ's hands and feet through brotherhood. He experiences love and acceptance maybe for the first time in his life, allowing a wounded heart to safely trust again.

This, combined with God's grace, takes a man's breath away as he wants to cry out: "Wow, you feel that way too? We really are all in this together." Such an atmosphere results in men wanting more of what they see modeled, surrendering to their loving God. That attractiveness is reinforced by a core group of brothers who offer acceptable, relatable, and sustainable Christlike relationships.

The measure of a man is in the strength of his surrender, as the measure of his surrender is in submission to and love for his brothers. Think of it this way: *How can a man truly surrender to God who is unseen without submitting in love to the spiritual authority and brothers God has laid before him on earth?*

Men who seek to know God's will must seek men who know God well. The common curse for the Christian man is isolation, which is the breeding ground for delusion. Men tend to be as sick as their secrets.

REASON# 3: A VEILED PERSPECTIVE OF THE MANHOOD OF JESUS CHRIST

Jesus Christ modeled perfect sonship as both God and man, not in moral muscle, but in the magnificent meekness (strength under control) of a submissive servant. As a man rightfully focuses on the deity of Christ, he may miss the lessons of our High Priest's indomitable humanity. The ability to pattern our own lives after his most outstanding attributes as a man is the apex of male discipleship.

Comparing ourselves to Christ's manhood can result in both success and failure. It results in failure if we try to measure up to his perfect courage, sacrificial love, and kindness toward others. But it results in success if we accept our failures and limitations, which blessedly opens the door to his power through a grace that enables our obedience.

When the veil is lifted and men see our Savior's manhood, they are granted permission to set a supernatural standard to follow, while walking in the grace that must precede that standard. Men are now free from the tyranny of comparing themselves to every other man on the planet. With Christ as our standard, we are less likely to exalt or diminish ourselves. Those who pride themselves because they are smarter, richer, or more gifted than another man will change their scorecards with Christ as their standard for manhood. And because we are heirs with Christ, those who think less of themselves will see their true value as a recipient of grace.

At this point in history, the light of biblical manhood is flickering and nearly extinguished, having largely sold out to cultural promises that never deliver. Restoring the masculine heart to the church of Christ is a daunting call whose only muscle is the Holy Spirit. I am grateful to God you have chosen to answer that call, this Great Commission called discipleship.

My friend, never forget the cry of Galatians 5:1: "It is for freedom that Christ has set us free." As teachers of men, we have a responsibility to model and magnify freedom by leading with the irresistible grace and the no-fault love of Christ.

34

MOBILIZING MEN TO MISSIONS

(GRAHAM GAMBLE)

Graham Gamble is the founder of 360 World Changers Ministry, equipping pastors and youth leaders to become more effective in helping others experience accelerated spiritual growth, putting their faith into practice through sharing the gospel, and making disciples who make disciples. Visit AdventureSportsMinistry.org or Facebook.com/360World Changers for more information.

> *And Jesus came up and spoke to them, saying, "All authority has been given to Me in heaven and on earth. Go therefore and make disciples of all the nations, baptizing them in the name of the Father and the Son and the Holy Spirit, teaching them to observe all that I commanded you." (Matthew 28:18–20 NASB)*

I t is estimated that of the 7.2 billion people alive today, 3 billion live in unreached people groups with little or no access to the Gospel of Jesus Christ. According to the Joshua Project, there are approximately 16,300 unique people groups in the world. Of these, 6,500 are considered unreached. The vast majority (95 percent) live in the 10/40 Window. Less than 10 percent of missionary work is done among these people.[1]

We expect a lot from Christian men today. They're supposed to be great husbands and fathers, provide financially for their families, serve as volunteers in their communities and their children's sports associations, and provide leadership at church. Despite all these distractions, Jesus commands us to go: "The eyes of the LORD range throughout the earth to strengthen those whose hearts are fully committed to him" (2 Chronicles 16:9). God will keep his promise, "Call to Me and I will answer you, and I will tell you great and mighty things, which you do not know" (Jeremiah 33:3 NASB), including new and creative ways to inspire men toward missions.

Current giving trends show that 87 percent of funds donated to missions goes to work among groups that are already Christian; 12 percent goes to work among people who live within reach of the gospel but have not responded; and only 1 percent goes toward work among unreached groups. According to the Joshua Project, most "unreached" people groups live in the poorest countries within the 10/40 Window. People in this region face extreme poverty, high levels of depression, female infanticide, human trafficking, and spiritual darkness and oppression. Men are the perfect tool to reach these hurting people.

God has placed in men's hearts a deep desire for purpose and fulfillment, and to influence the world around them—in short, a desire for the "abundant life" promised in John 10:10. Your job is to awaken this desire and uncover practical ways for men to engage that world. The book of James teaches us that having faith without putting it into practice leaves us feeling dead. Therefore, mobilizing men into missions is not only important for the sake of those they will be ministering to, but it is just as important for the ongoing spiritual health of those ministering.

Everything starts with prayer. If you want to see a change in the hearts and actions of the men in your care, get a few leaders together and spend some *extended* time in prayer. I do not mean praying for an hour. I mean praying for three hours, five hours, or better yet, all night. A mentor challenged me to do this for my own ministry in the fall of 2016. Here are some highlights.

As I prayed all night, I asked the Lord to expand my impact from the twenty or so youth I was influencing in Houston at the time to a hundred thousand. In just one year, we are now seeing large numbers of pastors and leaders in several countries training thousands with our 360 World Changers material. People are being transformed, churches are growing, and congregations are spreading the gospel for the first time. Two warring tribes in Africa began turning in their weapons and crying out to God for reconciliation.

None of this happened by accident. The power of God must be at work to have any impact in our world for the kingdom of God. Jesus promised that believers would receive power, through the Holy Spirit, to be his witnesses to the ends of the earth. Ask for an outpouring of the Spirit of God upon the men under your leadership for the purpose of ministry.

Men are goal-oriented creatures. They love to be challenged and inspired with a big vision about how they can make a significant difference in their world. Pastor John Piper said, "Every man feels a lack of satisfaction with just making money, paying the bills, playing golf. He's longing for an adventure bigger than himself. Something that gets juices flowing better than anything. God made him that way." Passion is contagious. As a leader of men, get educated about current needs around the world. If you are not passionate, you will not ignite a fire among your men.

Matthew 14:14 tells us, "When Jesus landed and saw a large crowd, he had compassion on them and healed their sick." That's just one of more than twenty times in the Gospels in which Jesus saw something, felt compassion, and was moved to act. Matt Bullen of Mission Critical International was the influence behind thirty-five kids being adopted in Colombia by simply inspiring people to go, see, and experience orphanages there. He writes:

> I arrived at that first orphanage in Colombia and I said to the Holy Spirit, "Oh, so *this* is where you've been working and waiting for me to show up." ... I had been an American pastor for twenty-five years and had never felt that feeling. ... Back home in the US, I started telling everyone who would listen about the amazing impact this experience had on me. ... In

the next seven years, I took twenty-five more trips to Colombia to bring others to feel what I felt and to see what I saw. That is the formula—we have to see what God sees, which causes us to feel his heart for the desperate, which causes us to feel compassion, which causes us to act.

The needs and opportunities are endless. You can begin sooner than you think. Right in your local community, the men in your charge—as a group or individuals—can feed the homeless, mentor a young person, build a home, reach out to refugees, and so on.

Lead a short-term mission trip in our own nation or overseas. Have your men work in an orphanage, build a school or church, conduct a vacation Bible school, dig a water well, or reach out to at-risk youth. Or think big. Schedule intense short- or longer-term trips that engage unreached people, provide disaster relief, establish medical missions, or combat human trafficking. As men get involved in missions, God will engage their hearts. They can then serve as a resource and inspiration to other men, fulfilling the call of 2 Timothy 2:2—to entrust what they have learned to faithful men who will then be equipped to teach others.

Global Frontier Missions points out, "We have found that short-term mission trips and summer internships are one of the greatest mobilization tools. We haven't found any better way to get people involved in God's global purposes than bringing people on a short-term mission trip so that they can see the need first hand."[2]

As a leader, you are in a unique position to mobilize men of God to be world changers; to give them a vision with a purpose. Educate yourself, travail in prayer for those under your leadership, inspire them to action, and engage their hearts through meaningful hands-on experiences. Challenge them, as Francis Chan says, to "try things that only succeed if God shows up."

RESOURCES

Information Websites

- Joshua Project: https://joshuaproject.net
- Operation World: http://www.operationworld.org

- Perspectives on the World Christian Movement: http://www.perspectives.org/, http://www.iamsecond.com
- Frontier Ventures (formerly US Center for World Missions): https://www.frontierventures.org/, https://www.unicef.org
- East West Ministries: http://www.eastwest.org/, https://worldoutreach.org
- OMF International(US): https://omf.org/us
- Pioneers USA: https://www.pioneers.org
- Living Water International: www.water.cc
- Frontiers USA: https://www.frontiersusa.org
- Wycliffe Bible Translators: https://www.wycliffe.org

Suggested Books

- *The Insanity of God* by Nik Ripken
- *Crazy Love* by Francis Chan
- *Let the Nations Be Glad* by John Piper
- *Operation World* by Jason Mandryk

35

BLUE-COLLAR EVANGELISM: HOW TO LEAD A GUY TO CHRIST

(BRODIE COOPER)

Brodie Cooper is the executive director of Blast & Cast Men's Ministries, an interdenominational outreach ministry that utilizes the common bonds of hunting and fishing to reach lost outdoorsmen. Find out more at www.blastandcast.org or join at www.facebook.com/BlastandCast.

*E*vangelism is a scary word. I've had five-minute conversations that contained fewer syllables. It sounds "churchy," super-spiritual, and, if I'm being honest, like something someone else should be doing—someone more skilled and more comfortable interacting with people. Maybe someone like a pastor, or maybe that salesman you know who can talk the paint off the walls. It's definitely not for someone like me, who feels more comfortable in the company of redfish than people.

But, as a follower of Jesus Christ, there's no avoiding his words in Matthew 28:18–20. We are commanded to go and make disciples. It helps me to remember that the men who physically heard Jesus give this commandment were regular guys like you and me. They were not gifted orators and lacked formal education. They could not rely on anything that came naturally to them, and instead relied on the power and movement of the Holy Spirit.

When Jesus gave that command, he did so knowing effective evangelism requires no special skills or training. It isn't easy, but God didn't create us merely to accomplish easy tasks. He always supplies our needs along the way.

I like to call this blue-collar evangelism. It's an approach to sharing your faith that requires you to get your hands dirty by caring about people, living life alongside them, continually sharing the gospel as best as you can, and investing time in them as needed. And it works. Here are the basic concepts that shape the blue-collar approach.

First, effective evangelism is both words and actions. Our words provide context for our actions, and our actions prove the substance of our words. The truth is that actions without words lack context. There are lots of generally nice people doing generally good things in this world, and society jumps at any chance to worship at the altar of humanity. Failing to give the gospel credit for the transformation in your life means you get the glory for it rather than God. You don't want to be the guy who steals God's glory, so be the guy who gives God glory by providing an explanation when someone notices how you approach life differently than the other guys on the job or in the neighborhood.

Likewise, words without actions are empty, meaningless, and often self-serving. Unfortunately, many so-called Christians preach a compromised gospel to benefit their egos or their pocketbooks. The gospel message is life changing by nature, so let your life-change provide evidence for the truth of your words.

Second, effective evangelism and instant success rarely go together. We live in a culture that demands everything *now*. Instant coffee. Microwave popcorn. On-demand television. We love immediate gratification, and that's usually what we expect when we share our faith. Most people get that queasy, oh-no-God's-telling-me-to-do-something feeling, awkwardly say something about Jesus, and then get shocked and surprised when there is little to no response.

Jesus provides us a picture of effective evangelism in the parable of the sower (see Matthew 13:1–9, 18–23). If our gospel seeds are ever going to grow and produce a harvest, we need to commit to doing a lot of work. It shouldn't come as a surprise when we need to spend years digging up rocks, cutting off thorns, and scaring away birds to get that dirt ready. If your golfing buddy needs help rooting out addiction or pride issues, get in there and help him. If your neighbor loves the things of the world more than he loves God, show him what it looks like to make tough, faith-filled decisions. If your business partner has relationship issues, model unconditional love and support.

Care enough to get your hands dirty. Commit to the long-term effort of evangelism by preparing the soil, consistently sowing gospel seeds with your words, and trusting that the harvest will come in due time.

Third, the goal of effective evangelism is to create a follower of Jesus, not someone who simply agrees with you. It's great to be able to say you led ten men in prayer to receive Jesus last year, but is that really success? How many of those men went on to become disciple-making followers of Jesus? How many later fell away because they still had too many rocks and thorns in their lives?

The American church desperately needs to redefine success when it comes to evangelism. Too often we set new believers up for failure because our goal in sharing with them is simply to lead them to a profession of faith. Jesus commanded us to go and make disciples, so our evangelism efforts should move someone past the profession of faith and into a day-to-day walk with Jesus.

When done well, the line between evangelism and discipleship is almost indistinguishable because we've prepared the soil and we've shown them what it looks like to follow Jesus over a lengthy period. If it takes a little more time to loosen that soil, take the time. Set them up for success as a follower of Jesus, rather than rushing them down the aisle.

Fourth, effective evangelism is a lifestyle, not a skill set. Though some are particularly gifted in this area, evangelism is not a skill set. You don't have to be Billy Graham. You don't have to be a pastor. You don't even have to be a people person. In fact, sometimes being an ordinary guy who isn't so good with words is a huge advantage. People value authenticity.

For the follower of Jesus, evangelism is a way of life. Here's what it looks like in ten steps, from planting the first seed to watching roots grow deep:

1. *Be purposeful in your relationships with those who don't know Jesus.* Your goal in every relationship—neighbors, coworkers, fishing buddies, or whoever—is to create followers of Jesus. Not just one person, but every person.

2. *Don't settle for shallow relationships … go deeper!* Ask open-ended spiritual questions. Invite people to church and outreach events hosted by men's ministries. Ask *why* a lot. Be vulnerable and open about yourself. Be willing to talk about your weaknesses. Don't limit relationships to work, sports, or small talk. Dig in!

3. *Share the gospel early and often, even if it's awkward.* When you ask that spiritual question and they show interest, give a short gospel presentation. When they ask about your past, include the gospel in your testimony. If it's awkward, they'll know it's important enough to you that you're willing to endure awkwardness to share.

4. *If you don't know the answer, tell them you don't know the answer.* It's okay to not know something. They ask questions because they don't know either. This is a chance to bring in a mentor or pastor, or invite them to a study group. You don't have to answer all their questions if you help them find someone who can.

5. *Dare to care deeply.* This can feel extremely vulnerable, but vulnerability and authenticity go hand in hand. It's personal. Jesus loved this person enough to die for him. As a follower of Jesus, allow yourself to begin caring about that individual in the same way.

6. *Pray. Pray again. And then pray some more.* You can't open the eyes of the blind or the ears of the deaf. You desperately need God to show up. Pray for words. Pray for opportunities to show that your words are true. Pray for eyes that see and ears that hear. Pray that the birds, rocks, and thorns would be uprooted so the gospel has room to grow.

7. *Be willing to do something no one else would ever be willing to do.* Be prepared to be the hands and feet of Jesus, even if it's really hard and really uncomfortable. It could mean a late-night hospital visit. It could mean peace, prayer, and counsel in the face of incredible difficulty. It could mean great personal sacrifice.

8. *Don't be afraid to do something that doesn't make sense.* God has a way of directing you to just the right word and to just the right action at just the right time. It might not make earthly sense, but that's often how God works. You've been praying for this chance, so you'll know it when you see it. Just follow!

9. *When they ask why, share the gospel again.* When they see that your life and actions don't make sense, they'll ask why. When they see love and faith in motion, they'll ask how. Tell them! Ask the Holy Spirit to speak and say what needs to be said. Don't hold back!

10. *Follow up and follow through.* No matter what their response may be, stay committed. Go back to the beginning if you need to, as many times as you need to. Keep helping them get their dirt ready. Keep digging out rocks and cutting off thorns. Bring them into fellowship with other Christians. Get in the Bible with them. Pray with them. Demonstrate what it means to follow Jesus. Be authentic and real.

Skills and formal training are great ways to polish your approach, but don't fall into the trap of thinking they are a necessity. Being a great speaker can actually make it easy to forget that you are utterly dependent on God's provision anytime you share your faith. Remember, Jesus sent out ordinary fishermen to reach the world and the results speak for themselves. If you're willing to love people enough to get your hands dirty, living life with them, then God is more than faithful to give you every word and every opportunity necessary.

Section VII

GROWING
YOUR
ORGANIZATION

36

SHOULD I GO INTO FULL-TIME MINISTRY?

(MIKE YOUNG)

Mike Young is the founder and director of Noble Warriors. He currently serves as president of the National Coalition of Ministries to Men. Mike and Stacy live in Chesterfield, Virginia, and have four children. Contact him at www.noblewarriors.com.

I often have conversations with men who are thinking about quitting their jobs and going into men's ministry full-time. These men come to me for advice because I left the business world and jumped into full-time ministry a decade ago.

Back in 2004, after much prayer and consideration, my wife, Stacy, and I felt certain about a call to full-time ministry to men. After a lengthy runway process, I quit my job and launched our ministry, Noble Warriors, in August of 2005.

We thought we were ready. We had saved a year's worth of living expenses for our family of six. We had no debt other than our mortgage. Our church was behind us. I brought an enormous sense of kingdom adventure and risk tolerance, which was balanced by a well-grounded, practical-minded accountant wife. We even bought a book to guide us: *The Nonprofit Kit for Dummies.*

We launched with big dreams but no real ministry plan. We had no plan for raising support. (I thought churches would throw money at our great idea!) We had no name recognition. (You should have heard some the early phone calls and visits: "Mike who?" "Noble what?") We had no history of ministry in the community beyond our own church. And we had no idea how to connect with local pastors and other leaders.

In hindsight, I now see how unprepared we were. Truth is, a lot of men go into full-time ministry unprepared. They launch with big dreams but no realistic plan to achieve those dreams. There are a lot of used-car salesmen who used to be men's ministers. Ministry to men is not for the faint of heart. I'm grateful to God for showing his favor to Noble Warriors. Despite our many missteps, the ministry has survived and thrived.

What should you do if you feel called to full-time men's ministry? Begin by "wrestling with your calling." I started my career as a high school science teacher and football coach. Five years in the classroom were followed by three years as a high school assistant principal. After eight years in education, God made it clear that I was to move on.

I joined my father-in-law's custom home-building business as a construction manager for large custom-home projects. I became an officer and partner in the business. Stacy and I thought that was our future. We planned to buy some land, build a dream home, and raise our family. But once again, I secretly felt the need for change, but I didn't know what, where, or how.

One day I came home from a construction site and Stacy said, "Mike, you're miserable. It's making me miserable, and I'm ready for a change." I was amazed that she sensed my unsettledness, but neither of us knew what to do next. So we prayed.

Months later, I heard a radio show hosted by Dr. James Dobson. His guests were Chris Van Brocklin, Vince D'Acchioli, and Patrick Morley. These men were from the National Coalition of Ministries to Men (NCMM). Their topic was how to disciple men. As I listened to these men, my heart was stirred.

A few weeks later, I attended my first NCMM gathering. Our leader was a man named Brian Doyle. He said, "I'd like to think there'll be a hundred more full-time men's ministry leaders in the country in the coming year." I didn't know who the other ninety-nine guys were, but I knew I was supposed to be one.

There were clear markers on my journey. The markers came early. As a young man, God gave me a supportive family, a dad who invested in my life, and an amazing series of encouragers and experiences that were all part of his preparation for my calling. I was saved by Christ as a teenager, but I was not discipled until well into adulthood. In addition to my parents, significant individuals built my faith along the way—these included high school coaches, a campus minister, a camp director, and several pastors.

Five years as a public-school teacher forced me to learn to communicate well, and three years as a high school assistant principal taught me much about organizational leadership and managing people. Seven years in construction taught me basic business skills and financial management. God gave me a generous spirit; I love to serve folks and give things away. Raising three sons has given me much to consider and pray over regarding building men. And I'm an extrovert, an idea generator, and an adventurous guy who loves a challenge and the unknown.

Your life story is unique too, and God has a unique plan for your life and ministry. But be cautious about jumping into vocational ministry if you don't have a clear sense of how God may have been preparing you, your marriage, and your family for this adventure.

When we launched, I imagined Noble Warriors would serve the entire Richmond, Virginia, metro region with men's ministry. But God said, "No, I'm not giving you that much." So I thought, *We'll serve all of Chesterfield County ... that's really scaled back.* And God said, "No, that's too big too."

Ultimately, we launched Noble Warriors by serving three churches that sat within five miles of each other. That was it. And thank God, I started small. Our humble beginning gave me opportunities to learn the business, make connections, develop skills, and face the challenges of helping churches build men. Here are a few factors that I think were critical to our early progress:

- God forced me to start small *and* serve my own church.
- We learned quickly by making many mistakes.

- Mature, godly friends and encouragers helped with basic needs.
- Veteran men's disciplers I met through NCMM were valuable resources for ideas, content, theology, and philosophy of discipling men.

Before you decide to pursue full-time ministry, here are a few questions to ask yourself:

- *Am I qualified?* If you feel called to men's discipleship but have never discipled a man one-on-one, led a men's small group, or spoken in front of a group of men, you've got some work to do.
- *Am I willing to serve where I'm already planted?* Start where you are and do everything you can. As God uses you to truly disciple men in your church and multiplies your ministry, other pastors and leaders will hear about it, and you'll have an opportunity to serve beyond your own flock.
- *Am I willing to learn from others?* Ask questions, read books about discipling men (contact me for some great recommendations), and connect with other ministry leaders and organizations.
- *Am I a supporter of the local church?* One of the reasons God has shown favor to Noble Warriors is that we continue to esteem the local church. I encourage you to do the same. As you serve your church and others, your ministry will grow. You may reach a point where the next step is to launch an organization.
- *Am I willing to market myself?* A lot of men are reluctant to promote their ministries out of a sense of humility. But if God has truly called you to serve him, you should promote your ministry with confidence and enthusiasm.
- *Do I have a heart for men, or do I desire the spotlight?* Sometimes men go into ministry because they fancy themselves great Bible teachers; they want an opportunity to be "the guy up front." If this is your motivation, you will crash and burn.

- *Am I willing to be patient as God grows my ministry?* Men's ministry is notoriously slow growing. Are you willing to persevere through the dry times?
- *Am I willing to do the administrative work?* Ironically, operating your own organization can decrease the amount of time you have for people. You've got paperwork, fundraising, event planning, writing, promotional work, corporate reporting, and year-end accounting. And don't forget exercise, sleep, and prayer.

I hope this has been helpful to you as you discern your next steps. Here are the two best pieces of advice I can give you. First, avoid launching an independent ministry unless you and your wife have incredibly strong confirmation that this is exactly what God wants you to do *and* you have a robust support system. Your wife must possess an unwavering resolve that this is God's calling for you *together* so she doesn't resent "your" decision when paychecks don't come consistently. (Stacy added this sentence.) And second, maximize your ministry potential while working your regular job and serving in your church and your community.

If you were hoping I would give you the green light to start your own ministry (or the red light), I'm sorry. God will honor your quest. He will bring clear guidance—in his time, not yours. In the meantime, feel free to contact me, or any active member of NCMM, to brainstorm ways God might be calling you to maximize your gifts, talents, and abilities.

Be encouraged. Trust God. Expect to find ministry opportunities around every corner. Then follow the instructions of Ecclesiastes 9:10: "Whatever your hand finds to do, do it with all your might." Finally, don't follow my example unless you're absolutely certain that launching a ministry is God's plan for your life.

37

TOOLS AND RESOURCES FOR MINISTRY TO MEN

(STEVE HOPPER)

Steve Hopper is the men's ministry representative for the EFCA (Evangelical Free Church of America) West District. He appreciates well-designed, engaging biblically based books and resources. Contact Steve at stv.hopper@gmail.com.

Having the right tools can make all the difference in the world—whether you're working on your car, repairing something at home, or helping another man become more like Jesus. Here is a peek inside my men's ministry toolbox. Depending on your location, goals, and resources, you'll want to identify ministries and resources that work for you. Because men are at different levels of maturity and readiness, consider offering opportunities to engage men at different levels of commitment.

TO GATHER MEN

Initiate a variety of entry-point opportunities for men to attend, such as one-time seminars on felt needs—like fathering (maybe "Great Dads") or how to be the husband your wife needs. Man in the Mirror offers events on a wide range of topics. Other examples include:

- Professional sporting events, like a minor-league baseball game
- Hearty men's breakfasts with a speaker

- Golf events
- Men's conferences and retreats
- Outdoor adventures like shooting, hunting, and fishing

For a great perspective, see "Entry Points—More Than a Pancake Breakfast" by Brian Doyle, in the book *Men's Ministry in the 21st Century* (Group Publishing).

TO CONNECT MEN

Capture the momentum from your outreach events by connecting men into a small group around God's Word. Here are some great tools:

Video and Audio Curriculum

Authentic Manhood: *33 The Series*™ inspires and equips men to pursue life as modeled by Jesus in the thirty-three years he lived on earth. Biblical teaching by a diverse team addresses issues important to men with a contemporary format, supported by testimonies, round-table discussions, and man-on-the-street interviews. Visit authenticmanhood.com for more information.

Men's Fraternity: This three-year study is the world's most popular men's ministry video series. "The Quest for Authentic Manhood" addresses wounds men experience and the biblical definition of manhood; "Winning at Work and at Home" provides practical teaching on two critical areas of a man's life; and "The Great Adventure" teaches men how to serve by identifying his unique design and gifting.

Lifeway's *Kingdom Man* by Tony Evans: This DVD and workbook is designed to give men understanding, vision, and perspective on their identity and responsibilities, along with practical steps on how to become a man who rules his world well. Visit lifeway.com/men for more information.

FamilyLife: *Stepping Up* (with Dennis Rainey) is a dynamic video series that challenges men to "step up" to manhood at every season of life. It includes a variety of great teachers, man-on-the-street testimonies, and vignettes. For more information, visit familylife.com.

Walk Thru the Bible Ministries: *Personal Holiness in Times of*

Temptation is a classic series by Dr. Bruce Wilkinson, helping men choose victory over sin and temptation. Also, *Crucible: The Choices that Change Your Life Forever* by Phil Tuttle follows David as he faces critical choices throughout his life and shows how faith, trust, fear, truth, despair, sacrifice, and humility draw him closer to the heart of God. Visit walkthru.org for more information about this series.

Family Matters: *Basic Training for a Few Good Men* by Tim Kimmel gives husbands and dads marching orders for moral and spiritual leadership in the key areas of family, work, community, and church—all delivered powerfully, with warmth and humor. Visit familymatters.net for more information.

Tyndale: *Quiet Strength* by Tony Dungy. This is a DVD study from a Super Bowl football coach on the principles, practices, and priorities of a winning life. Great for mentoring young men.

CBMC: *Operation Timothy* is great for one-on-one or group investigative Bible study on discipleship that includes workbooks and audio messages from great teachers. Visit operationtimothy.com for more information.

Navigators*: Every Man a Warrior* equips men through powerful testimony to develop lifelong habits of personal quiet time and Bible study. Visit everymanawarrior.com for more information.

Influencers: *The Journey* is a dramatic and compelling nine-month discipleship experience to help men "abide in Christ" and become self-feeding Christians. For more information, visit influencers.org.

Man in the Mirror: *Life Plans* (there are five to pick from) are short, six-week Bible studies with no work required between meetings. They work as a stand-alone or a follow-up to a men's seminar. *Man in the Mirror* is a weekly video Bible study series (mimbiblestudy.com) that has hundreds of Bible study videos, along with downloadable handouts, organized into short series.

No Regrets Men's Ministries: The *No Regrets Study Series* is especially for committed small groups. This comprehensive discipleship experience from Steve Sonderman and Elmbrook Church includes Bible study, Scripture memory, outside reading, and audio messages. Visit menwithnoregrets.org for more information.

BOOKS FOR GROUP STUDY

- *Point Man* by Steve Farrar
- *Tender Warrior* by Stu Weber
- *The Man in the Mirror* and other titles by Patrick Morley
- *Wild at Heart* and other titles by John Eldredge
- *The Measure of a Man* by Gene Getz
- *7 Men and the Secret of Their Greatness* by Eric Metaxas
- *Mansfield's Book of Manly Men* by Stephen Mansfield

LEADERSHIP TRAINING

- *Charting a Bold Course—Training Leaders for a 21st Century Ministry* by Andy Seide. This is a twenty-week leadership training manual.
- Center for Church Based Training. This is excellent for discipleship, leadership, and elder training curriculum (ccbt.org).
- *The Measure of a Man* by Gene Getz. This classic book focuses on character qualities for godly men as seen in 1 Timothy 3 and Titus 1. A video series is also available from Grace Ministries (grace101.org).
- *Brothers! Calling Men into Vital Relationships* by Geoff Gorsuch, with Dan Schaffer. This outstanding book helps small group leaders understand the unique dynamics of a men's small group.

SERVICE MINISTRY

New Commandment Men's Ministries: *Developing a Men's Team Ministry to Widows, Widowers, and Single Parents* is a training package that shows the men of your church how to "adopt" a widow, single mother, or others in need, to help with practical home repair and more. Visit newcommandment.org for more information.

TRAINING MEN'S MINISTRY LEADERS

How to Build a Life-Changing Men's Ministry is a ten-session DVD training series based on the groundbreaking book by Steve Sonderman (menwithnoregrets.org).

Sleeping Giant by Kenny Luck. Awaken the men in your church with this book and video training sessions by the former men's leader at Saddleback Church (lifeway.com).

Building a Ministry of Spiritual Mentoring by Jim Grassi. Wise counsel and a valuable "toolbox" full of resources from a veteran men's leader.

No Man Left Behind by Patrick Morley, David Delk, and Brett Clemmer. This boils down some of the typical "men's ministry" paradigms while developing an intentional strategy to reach and disciple men. (Live, online, and video versions available at nomanleftbehind.org.)

MINISTRY TO MEN

Why Men Hate Going to Church: This DVD includes full-length live audience presentations by David Murrow and insight from two leading pastors on how to get past the excuses and really impact men and boys. Based on Murrow's best-selling book (churchformen.com).

Men's Ministry in the 21st Century—The Encyclopedia of Practical Ideas. Proven strategies for fostering a strong, caring, welcoming, and engaging community of men in your church.

Pastoring Men by Patrick Morley. A must-read for every pastor. Don't miss "Seventy Things Every Man Needs to Know." Companion website has additional articles and teaching from author (visit pastoringmen .com for more information).

BOOKS FOR HUSBANDS

- *Guard Your Heart* by Gary Rosberg
- *Connecting with Your Wife* by Barbara Rosberg
- *52 Things Wives Need from Their Husbands* by Jay Payleitner
- *For Men Only* by Shaunti and Jeff Feldhahn
- *The Marriage Prayer* by Patrick Morley and David Delk

RESOURCES TO HELP MEN BE SPIRITUAL LEADERS IN THEIR HOMES

The Manger Build: Dad helps his kids build a life-size manger, and then leads a series of Christmas devotions. From Noble Warriors (themangerbuild.org).

Heritage Builders: *The Family Nights Bundle* features more than seventy ideas and activities to bring fun and spiritual growth to your family on a regular basis. Pass on a spiritual heritage with this unique resource from Otis Ledbetter, Jim Weidman, and Kurt Bruner (heritage builders.com).

"Sticky Faith": Vital research-based strategies to help parents and churches raise kids who will "stick" with their faith when they leave home. Including books, kits, and DVD series (stickyfaith.org).

"Letters from Dad": A plan for men to develop letters communicating their hearts to their wife and children. From Grace Ministries (grace101.org).

Faith@Home: Mark Holmen has developed helpful books and DVD training for intentional Deuteronomy 6 parenting (faithat home.com).

"Rite of Passage": Equip men to lead their sons into manhood. *Spiritual Milestones* by Jim and Janet Weidmann (Heritage Builder Books). See also Chuck Stecker, A Chosen Generation Ministries (achosengeneration.info) and Robert Lewis, *Raising a Modern-Day Knight* and the companion DVD study (rmdk.com).

BOOKS FOR BEING THE SPIRITUAL LEADER IN YOUR HOME

- *Point Man* by Steve Farrar
- *Tender Warrior* by Stu Weber
- *52 Things to Pray for Your Kids* by Jay Payleitner
- *The Power of Teachable Moments* by Jim Weidmann

SPEAKERS FOR DADS

"Great Dads": This excellent half-day seminar will come to your church. It is very affordable and doable. Includes a six-week follow-up study (visit greatdads.org, and then click on Seminars).

"Be the Dad": Best-selling author Jay Payleitner uses personal stories, biblical truths, and cultural touchpoints to deliver dad-friendly strategies (visit jaypayleitner.com for more information).

"Family Devotions that Blow Up the Box": Author and longtime youth worker Tim Shoemaker demonstrates how you can teach kids truth and hold their attention—even teens—with easy, powerful, and sometimes crazy object lessons (visit timshoemakersmashedtomatoes .com for more information).

BOOKS FOR DADS

- *Raising a Modern-Day Knight* by Robert Lewis and Dennis Rainey
- *52 Things Kids Need from a Dad* by Jay Payleitner
- *Grace-Based Parenting: Raising Kids for True Greatness* by Tim Kimmel
- *Passing the Baton: 100 Life Principles & Life Skills Every Father Needs to Teach* by Grady Hauser
- *Interviewing Your Daughter's Date* by Dennis Rainey
- *The Dad in the Mirror* by Patrick Morley and David Delk
- *Dad, If You Only Knew* by Josh and Jim Weidmann
- *Give Them Wings* by Carol Kuykendall

FOR DADS OF JUNIORS
OR SENIORS IN HIGH SCHOOL

College Ready: This is a six-part DVD series from FamilyLife, featuring Dennis Rainey and Robert Lewis (collegeready.com).

The Truth Project from Focus on the Family. This is an in-depth Christian worldview DVD series to prepare you and your teen (the truthproject.org).

Just One More Thing: Before You Leave Home by David Gudgel. Thirty short, practical chapters to review with your son or daughter over breakfast or lunch. On money, roommates, moral dilemmas, and more (visit davidandbernice.com for more information).

CONSULTING AND COACHING

Men's Ministry Catalyst: Founded in 1981 by Jim Grassi, this national ministry and team of coaches has helped thousands of churches to develop effective men's ministries. Find downloadable resources at mensministrycatalyst.org.

Man in the Mirror offers coaching and training through regional representatives. Check out their resources and articles at maninthe mirror.org.

MEN'S CONFERENCES

Men with No Regrets: Conference provides top speakers and offers host-site simulcast to local churches, prisons, and college campuses (menwithnoregrets.org).

Iron Sharpens Iron offers one-day men's conferences around the country with nationally known speakers, breakout workshops, and resources (ironsharpensiron.net).

CONCLUSION

Don't think you have to start from scratch to create memorable events, small-group curriculum, and leadership training material. Many of the above resources will match your exact goals, and others can be easily adapted for your ministry. Online searches to ministry websites will open doors to the very latest books and downloadable curriculum—but don't overlook the classics. Regional ministries and denominations also have a wide range of resources and annual gatherings for you to consider.

The above list is by no means exhaustive. It's simply the resources that have worked for me and some of my close colleagues. Members of the National Coalition of Ministries to Men (ncmm.org) are constantly brainstorming and creating new strategies for helping you reach the men in your church, your community, and beyond.

Finally, if you find something that works, share it with the ministry leaders in your region and your fellow ministry leaders at NCMM.

We're all in this together.

38

NONPROFIT VOLUNTEER TAX TIPS

(JEFF BUTCHER)

Jeffrey K. Butcher is national president of the Anglican Episcopal Men's Ministry program under the Brotherhood of St. Andrew, Louisville, Kentucky. Jeff spent twenty-eight years in the securities business and is a retired US Air Force lieutenant colonel, serving as a combat historian and public affairs officer. Contact Jeff at jeff.butcher@brothersandrew.net or visit brothersandrew.net.

As a volunteer, board member, or participant in your men's ministry, you may be able to legally deduct some of the expenses related to your ministry. I've become somewhat of an expert in these matters. Let me start you off with two questions:

1. Is your organization a bona fide IRS defined 501(c)(3) entity? If yes, then proceed to read on. If no, stop reading and find out why it is not.
2. Are you working with a Certified Public Accountant (CPA) or an Enrolled Agent (EA) who specializes in nonprofits? If not, then find one now.

DOES MY ORGANIZATION QUALIFY FOR TAX EXEMPTION?

If you lead a nonprofit ministry but haven't yet gotten a determination letter from the IRS, you'll want to do that right away. Filing for nonprofit status is a pain, but once your nonprofit is approved, you can deduct your expenses, save on sales tax, and accept gifts to pay for ministry expenses (and the gifts are tax-deductible for the contributor). If you are a small organization and want to skip the hassle of creating a nonprofit entity, you can join as Ministry Alliance (an NCMM member). They take care of all the IRS reporting and serve as a collection point for your donations.

Either way, the local Treasury District Office can also give you a separate letter confirming the 501(c)(3) status, which will include your tax identification number (TIN). I would suggest inserting it in a document protective sheet. Carry it with you always. Scan it and keep it on your hard drive. If you lose this number, it's hard to get it back. Your organization may be qualified as a religious organization or as a public benefit organization. Your letter will tell you which category you fit.

HOW CAN MY IRS LETTER BE USED?

As a nonprofit organization, many states will waive the sales tax on items you purchase for your organization. Your IRS determination letter is the proof the state will need to grant you sales tax exemption.

You should also use a separate credit card dedicated to your volunteer efforts. No personal expenses should ever be charged to this card. Your major credit companies, like American Express, Visa, Discover, and Master Card, will give you an end-of-the-year breakout by category for you at no extra charge. This is supporting data for your Excel spreadsheet. Your CPA or EA will love it.

Depending on your travel commitment, you should consider obtaining a dedicated rewards number through Marriott, Starwood, Holiday Inn, and Hilton, and so on for your nonprofit. I recently hosted twenty-five executive board members at a Hampton Inn. Each board member sent me a separate check for his room. In turn, the Hilton chain waived the sales taxes on each room using the organization's TIN. My nonprofit rewards card booked all the points because I used our dedicated credit card to pay all the room charges. This transaction produced two savings: no sales tax plus points toward a free night of lodging down the road with this hotel chain.

DEDUCTIONS FOR YOUR VOLUNTEERS AND BOARD MEMBERS

In general, volunteers should not expect to gain any tax advantages from their work with your ministry. Their investment of time and energy may be the lifeblood of your ministry, but for the most part only their travel and direct out-of-pocket expenses can be tax deductible. That's even more reason you should regularly show your appreciation to your board members and volunteers. A simple thank-you note is always appropriate. People like to feel appreciated, but how often do we use those words "Your efforts are most appreciated"? In addition, you might try some de minimis gift items to let them know you care.

According to Stephen Fishman, author of *Every Nonprofit's Tax Guide*, "In contrast to certain unreimbursed out-of-the-pocket expenses, unpaid volunteers may never deduct as a charitable contribution the value of their time or services, or the value of the income they lost while volunteering."[1] When you share a de minimis gift or offer ways to save on taxes, you could be winning a supporter for life.

KEEPING GOOD RECORDS

As a commission-only salesperson for twenty-eight years, I learned early on that keeping accurate and thorough records keeps the IRS at bay. A nonprofit volunteer can take advantage of several legal deductions if he follows the rules.

IRS Publication 463, "Travel, Entertainment, Gift, and Car Expenses," is a great starting point. Track your ministry-related expenses on an Excel spreadsheet with various categories on the left-hand side. This could include publications, supplies, computer equipment, alliance memberships, educational events (NCMM), lodging, food, transportation, parking, and airfare. Across the top is the monthly dividers, January to December, plus a column titled "Sum."

Sheet two of the Excel spreadsheet are your car expenses: starting miles, January 1, and ending odometer mileage, December 31. Go to page 27, Table 5-2, IRS PUB 463 for a good example. You could also include gas, maintenance, and possibly depreciation here. Currently, each mile to participate or promote is worth a fourteen-cent refund.

You do like refunds, right? Ask your CPA or EA what his or her preferences are in record keeping. A word of caution: Do not go cheap here by using Quicken or an independent agent to guide you. If you are so lucky as to encounter an audit down the road, you will know what I am talking about.

The mileage considerations could include going to a meeting across town, getting groceries for cooking breakfast or a special event, or attending a regional or statewide gathering for men's ministry. The mileage back and forth is all a potential tax deduction, plus the cost of the food if you bought it to feed the group.

In our denomination, we have an annual convention at different locations in the diocese. Should you be chosen to represent your men's ministry, you have several out-of-pocket nonreimbursable items you could claim: mileage, registration fee (meals included), materials' cost to develop booth, and lodging. If your national office has brochures or other handout material that are given to you for distribution, these, too, can be claimed should the office charge you for them, plus shipping. Always check the organization's guidelines for such events to make sure you do not file a claim in error. Some organizations will reimburse you for some expenses that others might not. Be advised that double dipping can cause the IRS to frown on you.

Uniforms are another possible refund claim. Some organizations will encourage their volunteers to wear a polo shirt with their logo on it when a person is working a public event. The volunteer can write off the shirt and matching pants, while not seeking any reimbursements. Cleaning these items is also permissible. Other possible items could include logo pins, nametags, and/or caps.

Publications and books on specific ministries related to a person's calling are also eligible. We live in an ever-changing world, and keeping up-to-date on innovations, trends, and useful information has become quite compelling.

Sponsorship and membership dues are another tax deduction. Alliance partners such as NCMM offer every one of us an opportunity to form relationships that are mutually beneficial for each partner—and we can deduct membership fees from income.

Finally, don't miss some of the free benefits that Microsoft and Google are offering nonprofits. These programs are for nonprofits with a valid TIN who are a 501(c)(3). Please visit microsoft.com /en-us/philanthropies/product-donations/default.aspx. For our religious nonprofit, we found an ability to upgrade the leadership team members to Microsoft Office 2016 for a one-time fee of twenty-nine dollars per person. It can be a lengthy process, but it is well worth the time.

Google has another host of actions you can take as well. In this case, search for "G Suite for nonprofits" (support.google.com/nonprofits). Google registration introduces you to Microsoft Office 2016, Symantec Security, and PhilanTech (an easier way to find new funding). Additional services consist of refurbished computers at a discount with free shipping; Glassdoor job listings; Fox Den online meeting service; QuickBooks; disaster recovery guide; and online TechSoup courses; and classes in grant writing. Each add-on can have a fee.

A host of other resources are also available, including IRS bulletins, business publishers, and apps for free or low-cost download.

IRS Publications:
- 463 Travel, Entertainment, Gift, and Car Expenses
- 526 Charitable Contributions
- 529 Miscellaneous Deductions
- 535 Business Expenses
- 557 Tax-Exempt Status for Your Organization
- Schedule A; 2106 Pubs Instructions
- IRS Form 2106-EZ Unreimbursed Employee Business Expense
- 4630 IRS.gov Exempt Organizations Product U Services Guide

Some websites for more information regarding tax tips include:
- www.irs.gove/charitaties-&-non-profits
- www.irsvideos.gove/nonprofits
- www.nolo.com/legal-encyclopedia/remind-nonprofit -volunteers-tax-Deductions-29659.html

- www.nonprofitfundraisingblog.com/2008/04/tax-deduction
  -advice-for-your.html

Nolo's *Every Nonprofit's Tax Guide*, 4th edition, by Stephen Fishman is helpful too.

Apps for iPhone and Android for keeping mileage expenses will vary depending on your computer capability and basic IT needs. Here are five for your consideration: Trip Log, Mileage Log Tracks; Trip Log 2.0 Mileage; Mileage Log GPS; Hurdlr-1099 Tax; and Miles-Automatic Mileage Log.

While this information is not meant to be exhaustive on starting a 501(c)(3) or covering all the tax tips that are eligible to ministries, hopefully these few tips will get you started on important tax savings and benefits for nonprofit ministries.

39

KEYS TO MINISTRY GROWTH AND SUSTAINABILITY

(C. MARSH BULL)

C. Marsh Bull is founder and president of Men's Group Foundation, Inc., a 501(c)(3). Find out more at mensgroup.org or contact Marsh at mensgrouptopics@gmail.com.

While the starting point for all ministry growth is committing ourselves and our labors to the Lord for his purposes and his glory, the key to *sustaining* a ministry is a long-term plan. The challenge facing all ministries (especially new ones) is getting leaders' and management's heads above day-to-day tactical tasks.

Planning may seem less important than holding a successful men's event, increasing sales of men's resources, or creating a new social-media campaign. But by gradually moving beyond a yearly focus, you will develop a much stronger organization. You can then grow faster and become financially stronger. Eventually, you will avoid the demanding pull of a short-term outlook where it seems you "never have any time" to plan for the future.

I recommend the "Critical Success Factor" plan or CSF plan. This document quickly addresses major opportunities and issues. The concept has been used for over forty years in the for-profit sector. Personally, I have been using CSF plans to work with nonprofits for more that fifteen years.

The typical time frame for a CSF plan covers fifteen to eighteen months, and, for those on a calendar year, it is usually created in the summer for implementation in early October. This timing schedule allows a CSF plan to drive a much more "proactive approach" to positioning an organization for success in the coming year.

The simplicity of this CSF approach is that it only asks, What are the five or six things the organization *must do* in the next fifteen to eighteen months? It identifies critical to-dos in driving growth, achieving financial stability, attaining long-term sustainability, and creating key performance measurement goals. Tasks are identified in detail and supported by specific action items agreed to by the board and senior management.

It is not easy changing from a year-to-year management mentality to taking a more long-term outlook. First attempts to develop a CSF plan typically elicit responses such as, "We don't have the time and resources," or, "There is too much going on—maybe next year."

To change from conducting business on a short-term basis, a men's ministry needs to start sometime, somewhere. A targeted CSF plan can "jump-start the organization" down the path of escaping a year-to-year survival mind-set and keep everyone focused.

To get started, below are critical success factors common to most nonprofits and men's ministries. You can add or replace these with ones unique to you:

1. Synchronize organizational direction with the vision and mission.
2. Transform from a "founder-focused" to a "sustainable 501(c)(3)" organization.
3. Increase revenue with diversified fundraising plan.
4. Deepen major customer relationships.
5. Focus marketing efforts and the power of branding.
6. Identify CSFs unique to "your" ministry.

CSF #1: Synchronization of the "current organizational direction" with the vision and mission is critical for long-term viability. The vision and mission should drive everything the organization does.

Whenever a men's ministry considers new services, products, or partnerships, the ideas need to be validated as supporting the vision and mission of the organization.

Organizations should review their vision and mission annually. If this isn't done, there is a tendency to wander into areas not originally planned. The for-profit world calls this scope creep, which is moving away from your intended purpose. Following are suggested to-dos:

- The board/organization leader must review the vision and mission, verifying they are accurate. If not, they must rethink them, pray, and change them as appropriate.
- Establish a mission and vision review step to ensure all new projects, services, and partnerships align.
- Verify the vision provides "strategic direction," including what the organization wants to achieve in the future. A vision should be big, like our God.
- Verify the mission describes the "organization's purpose and what their business is." For example, a ministry may have the mission of "providing small-group resources to churches."

It is especially important that the vision *not* be constrained by our human thoughts and ideas. God thinks much bigger than we do. Please don't restrain the potential godly impact your ministry can realize in reaching men by limiting your dreams and prayers.

Scripture commends the church to hold a bold mind-set. Ephesians 3:20 says, "Now to him who is able to do immeasurably more than all we ask or imagine, according to his power that is at work within us." I pray that as men's ministry leaders, we will personally be on fire for the Lord and do the same for our ministries.

CSF #2: Moving from a founder-focused to a sustainable 501(c)(3) organization is a critical challenge for many nonprofits, even though they may have been in existence for several years. There are two primary reasons. The first is the strong personality and drive of the founder; the second is the lack of a strong and effective board.

The board owns the major responsibility for the success of the nonprofit, not the founder. This may come as a surprise to many organizations, but it is essential for long-term organizational growth and sustainability. Following are suggested to-dos:

- Conduct basic board training, including fiduciary responsibilities. (Google for basic training ideas.) Recruit new board members and focus on increasing diversity.
- Ensure that at least one new board member has fundraising experience.
- Conduct at least three formal board meetings a year. (In February, review previous year's performance; in August, review first-half performance; in November, finalize next year's plan.)
- Develop yearly goals and objectives for the organizational leader by December 1 of each year.
- Empower the board to request periodic "State of Affairs" reports.

Implementing strong board governance does not take place overnight, but it is important to get underway for developing a strong board in order to become a sustainable 501(c)(3).

CSF #3: Increase revenue through an annual fundraising plan with diversified funding resources, including an annual monetary target. The plan must focus fundraising efforts on identifying, qualifying, and developing both current and new sources of revenue.

There are people and organizations that will want to support you. Your challenge is to find them. Following are suggested to-dos:

- Identify a goal for the following year, including cash, in-kind donations, will/bequeaths, and stocks.
- Categorize sources for donations, including current supporters, lapsed donors, and new donors, such as individuals, other organizations, service clubs, foundations, and government.
- Specifically identify a person for retaining and growing your "current supporter" base.

- Create a "talking points" document for fundraising that easily communicates the values *and* accomplishments of the organization.
- Identify new fundraising ideas, such as facility/program tours, get-to-know-us events, silent and/or live auctions, sponsorships, community events, and best practices of other men's ministries.
- Apply for 501(c)(3) grants. Using a Google Ad Grant (free advertising), the Men's Group Foundation increased website visits more than 500 percent and Bible study downloads more than 400 percent in a two-month period.

Accept that financial sustainability takes time, and know that other CSFs impact this area too.

CSF #4: Strengthen customer relationships. They are responsible for your success and existence, and they are the reason you are in business, the *ministry* business. There are numerous customer relationship programs available, but most of them are overkill for most men's ministries. Success in serving, growing, and retaining customers starts with recognizing their criticality. Many times, we get wrapped up in new services/markets and forget we first need to take care of our customers. Following are suggested to-dos:

- Customers need to be told by your ministry on a regular basis that they are important, greatly appreciated, and valued. Assign someone specifically to this task.
- Do you know who your real customers are? It can be confusing since you have clients, supporters, partners, and service users. Verify your true customer's definition.
- Identify why important customers come back to you, use your services, and value you.
- Survey customers at least once a year with general and specific questions. Don't take more than five minutes of their time. Use a tool such as SurveyMonkey (surveymonkey.com) to complete this task.

- Ensure you are up front and honest with your customers. If you aren't, they will find out.
- Develop stronger relationships with your customers. Create new ways of reaching out in a deeper way so customers believe they are special, needed, and appreciated.

CSF #5: Refine your marketing efforts and strengthen your brand image. The first step is acknowledging that these efforts are of strategic importance in fundraising, growth, and social-media presence.

Regarding marketing, ask, What is the prime message we need our customers, community, donors, and prospective donors to hear? For branding ask, What enables us to differentiate ourselves in our markets to attract and retain customers? When someone sees your name or logo, what does it mean to them, what do you stand for, and why are you a valued ministry? Following are suggested to-dos:

- For the upcoming year, what is the prime message we want to convey to our supporters, community, donors, and prospective donors? (Focus on your strongest values and benefits.)
- Create a simple marketing plan, or review and refine your current plan to drive awareness.
- Create or refine your target market in each area. Who is interested in or has a passion for what you do, and who has the propensity and means to donate meaningful resources?
- Don't focus the message on money or resource needs; rather, focus on your values and benefits.
- Benchmark with other men's ministries for new marketing and branding ideas.
- Conduct a simple survey to gather people's recognition and reaction to your name and logo.

Your critical success factor plan starts you down the path of growing your ministry, attaining financial strength, and achieving long-term sustainability.

Section VIII

KEEPING
YOURSELF
STRONG

40

YOUR FIRST MINISTRY
IS YOUR FAMILY

(JOSH MCDOWELL)

Josh McDowell is an international speaker, apologist, and author or coauthor of more than 140 books, including *More than a Carpenter* and *Evidence that Demands a Verdict*.

The phone rang. The person on the other end sounded depressed. "Josh, I need your help," Brad stated bluntly. "Emily and I are drifting apart, and I'm not motivated to do much about it." We agreed to meet for breakfast.

Emily and Brad had been married for eight years. Both attended church regularly and were thought of as mature Christians and strong leaders in our small community. Brad got right to the point. "Emily and I had a little argument last night, and I said something that really hurt her. After things had cooled down a bit, we were getting ready for bed when she just put it out there. 'Brad, do you love me anymore?'

"And, Josh, I waited for the longest time to answer and then finally just said, 'I don't know, Em. I just don't know anymore.' I know it's not right, but things have grown cold between us. I'm afraid both of us seem to have lost the motivation to get our marriage back on track."

What was developing between Brad and Emily was emotional distance. Their relationship was growing cold and their marriage was becoming stale. Brad was looking for something to spark his motivation to salvage a marriage that was going south. As I probed, I learned that nothing major had happened recently between him and Emily to make it worse. They simply seemed to have drifted apart.

I put down my cup of coffee, leaned toward Brad, and spoke softly. "How's your spiritual life, Brad?" I asked. "Do you feel close to God? Are you praying regularly for Emily? Do you long to please God like you used to?"

The expression on Brad's face told me he was puzzled by my questions. With a little irritation in his voice, he said, "I've got a relational problem with Emily, not a spiritual problem with God. Yes, I'm okay with him—it's Emily I'm struggling with."

MARRIAGE: A THREE-WAY PROPOSITION

Many couples—even mature Christians and ministry leaders—have bought into a common misconception about marriage. They think an intimate love relationship in marriage is primarily the result of the horizontal relationship between a husband and wife. They feel that each one has the responsibility to love the other, remain committed, and energize their motivation to keep their love life alive and well.

But marriage isn't just a horizontal relationship—it's also a vertical relationship. Marriage is a relationship between a man, a woman, and God. From the very beginning, God intended marriage to be a three-way proposition. He created a male in his image; he created a female in his image. And then he invited them to join him in his perfect circle of relationship—the triune Godhead of Father, Son, and Holy Spirit.

God's purpose all along was for humans to enjoy an intimate relationship with him. He didn't create the first couple and say, "Okay, I've created you two as relational beings, so go off in the garden and relate—I'm out of here!" No, he wanted to be a partner in this relationship called marriage.

Jesus was asked if a man could divorce his wife for any reason:

"Haven't you read the Scriptures?" Jesus replied. "They record that from the beginning 'God made them male and female.' And he said, 'This explains why a man leaves his father and mother and is joined to his wife, and the two are united into one. Since they are no longer two but one, let no one separate them, for God has joined them together." (Matthew 19:4–6 NLT)

God is the binding agent within a marriage. With his power and love, he is present so that the two joined as one may discover and delight in what he is all about—relationships. He created marriage, and he will be an active partner with a married couple if they will allow him. He is there in your marriage! And he feels the pain of any couple, like Brad and Emily, whose love for each other grows cold.

This may sound strange to you, but when you neglect your spouse and emotionally hurt the one you love, you also cause pain to another love of your life—Jesus. He loves your spouse as much as he loves you, and he feels his or her pain because he is part of your marriage relationship.

I wanted Brad to realize that when he was caring for and loving his wife, it was like caring for Jesus. I wanted Brad to realize that marriage is a three-way proposition. Jesus was there loving Brad's wife with tender care but was doing it alone because Brad had drifted away from her emotionally. And he was failing to meet Emily's deep needs on a human level.

It was as if Jesus were saying to Brad, *I was emotionally hungry, and you didn't feed me. I was emotionally thirsty, and you didn't give me anything to drink. I was emotionally vulnerable and naked, and you left me alone. I was emotionally sick, and you didn't come to my aid. Because when you began to abandon Emily in her emotional need, it was as if you were abandoning me.*

That idea should be a powerful motivation for any husband or wife. It is a thrilling thought that we delight Jesus when we minister to our spouses.

YOUR MINISTRY VERSUS YOUR MARRIAGE

Early in my ministry, Dottie traveled with me from city to city. She enthusiastically embraced my speaking ministry, and in many ways, she was my partner in ministry. But as we began to have children, it became difficult for her to be on the road with me. So she settled down in one place to make the "McDowell home" while I kept a packed schedule of traveling all over the country.

Dottie was fine with this arrangement, because she understood what my speaking ministry was all about—but it wasn't easy on her. I had told her to speak up anytime my schedule put too much of a strain on her. And one day she did.

I must admit I struggled a little with my loyalties. I wanted to be there for Dottie, while at the same time keeping God first in my life. How was I going to keep making him a priority in ministry and still attend to the needs of my family? After much deliberation, I decided *God had to come first and my family second.*

I'm sure glad I had chosen to make myself accountable to a few wise and more mature men who gave me wise counsel. My accountability partners helped me understand a few passages of Scripture about putting God first in my life.

The apostle Peter tells us, "You husbands must give honor to your wives. Treat your wife with understanding as you live together. ... Treat her as you should so your prayers will not be hindered" (1 Peter 3:7 NLT). And Jesus said, "You must love the LORD your God with all your heart, all your soul, and all your mind ... [and] love your neighbor as yourself" (Matthew 22:37–39 NLT). The apostle John wrote, "Dear children, let's not merely say that we love each other; let us show the truth by our actions" (1 John 3:18).

It took me back a little at first to think that if I didn't treat Dottie with honor and understanding, my prayers would be hindered. That was a big deal to me. I also realized that loving God with my everything was directly tied to loving my neighbor—and my wife was my closest neighbor. Finally, my love for Dottie couldn't just be words spoken on a long-distance call; I had to put my love into action.

It didn't take long to see that God wanted Dottie and my family not to come *before* my ministry, but that they *were my first ministry.* Showing love and care to her and the kids became my platform to minister to others. Putting God first was lived out and expressed in loving and attending to my closest neighbor, my wife.

This new perspective changed everything for me. I didn't stop traveling, but my speaking and ministry took on a whole new dimension. Loving and caring for my wife and children first made my work richer and more vibrant. Living with the woman I loved in an understanding way kept my prayers from being hindered. Together God, Dottie, and I began to make a great marriage, and my ministry actually became *more* effective.

Dottie and I still enjoy a great marriage. That isn't to say I still don't struggle with demonstrating my commitment to her while maintaining a busy schedule—I do. But it makes all the difference in the world when I see that God wants me to love him with my everything and love my closest neighbor (Dottie) as myself.

God wants your marriage to be rich and fulfilling too. He also wants your ministry to be rich and fulfilling. By now I trust you know my recommendation on how to organize your priorities. Pursue your relational journey with Christ with all your heart and strength. Then invite him to be the center point of your love life and marriage. Out of the overflow of those relationships, you will have more than enough fortitude, passion, and personal resources to pursue the ministry work to which God has called you.[1]

41

THE DEMAS DILEMMA: HOW TO SURVIVE WHEN YOU'RE ABANDONED AND BETRAYED

(BILL TERRY)

Bill serves as the men's ministries director for the International Pentecostal Holiness Church and the National Coordinator for Disaster Relief USA (DRUSA). Bill is also the acting president for Advantage College located in Northern California. He can be contacted at bterry@iphc.org.

As a pastor and a leader of men, I have experienced the pain of investing in the lives of men, only to see them leave the church and return to the ways of the world. Some have spoken ill of me and have even tried to discredit my ministry. This is not a new problem. The New Testament tells the story of a man named Demas, who abandoned his faith and pursued a worldly lifestyle.

Demas is mentioned three times in Scripture. In the first two passages, found in Colossians and Philemon, the apostle Paul refers to Demas as *a fellow worker*. However, the third passage describes him in this way: "Be diligent to come quickly; for Demas has forsaken me, having loved this present world, and has departed for Thessalonica" (2 Timothy 4:9–10 NKJV).

Demas had an amazing spiritual pedigree. He was mentored by

two men, who together wrote about half the New Testament: the apostle Paul and Luke the physician (who penned both the book of Acts and the Gospel that bears his name). Yet Demas' ministry season with godly mentors was not sufficient to keep him from falling away and choosing a different path. The words Paul used ("Demas has forsaken me") indicates both the disappointment and the pain he felt when the desires of this world pulled one of his protégés into its clutches.

Paul makes it clear why Demas fell away: "having loved this present world," Demas' attraction to glamour and glory became stronger than his promise and commitment to being a faithful Christ follower. Demas could not stand strong when the world came calling. He caved in, plunging into a world of temporary pleasure and fantasy.

The spirit of Demas is alive in the church today. As a men's minister, you know what I'm talking about. You mentor a man for years, pouring your life into him. You watch him grow and mature in the faith. And then one day, he's gone. He won't return your calls. Sometimes he abandons not only the church but his family as well. Sometimes he even turns on you.

Compare Demas to another hero of the faith: Moses. Like Demas, Moses encountered worldly temptations but handled them differently. Hebrews 11:24–26 says, "It was by faith that Moses, when he grew up, refused to be called the son of Pharaoh's daughter. He chose to share the oppression of God's people instead of enjoying the fleeting pleasures of sin. He thought it was better to suffer for the sake of Christ than to own the treasures of Egypt, for he was looking ahead to his great reward" (NLT).

Why was Moses able to conqueror his temptations while Demas succumbed? Here are four phrases that stand out from Hebrews 11:24–26:

1. "When he grew up …" Moses matured through the challenges in his life to eventually become a man of faith.
2. He "refused to be called the son of Pharaoh's daughter." Once Moses realized his true identity, he never wavered from his path to destiny.

THE DEMAS DILEMMA | 219

3. "He chose …" Moses made good choices.
4. "He was looking ahead …" Moses knew he had a future and a reward that was worth dying for.

Demas did exactly the opposite. Second Timothy 4:10 says, "Demas has forsaken me, having loved this present world, and has departed for Thessalonica" (NKJV). Demas' spiritual maturity, or lack thereof, is quite evident because his love for God was not nearly as strong as his love for the world. When the lure of the world came calling, Demas was not able to say no. Even with spiritual giants as mentors, Demas made poor choices; he could not see the greater future that awaited him. He was not able to see past the temporary pleasures of this life.

If you minister to men, it won't be long before you find yourself in the Demas dilemma. You will be abandoned or even betrayed by one of the men you serve. You will experience disappointment, grief, and rejection. You may even be tempted to abandon your ministry to men and go volunteer in the church parking lot. Don't do it! Paul didn't quit when he was betrayed. He kept fighting the good fight—and so must you.

Here are some practical tips on how to deal with your own Demas dilemma:

How do you win back a Demas who has fallen away?

Theodore Roosevelt has been quoted as saying, "Nobody cares how much you know, until they know how much you care." Start by showing genuine care for a fallen brother (see Galatians 6:1).

- Presence: A personal visit could make a huge difference.
- Concern: Chat with him on social media, but don't overdo it.
- Communicate: Just hearing a caring voice on the telephone can't hurt.
- Do something: Maybe invite your Demas to a nonspiritual event or activity, such as a baseball game. Don't mention his unfaithfulness; let the Spirit convict his heart. Remember, he must know that you love *him*, not just his presence at your Bible study.

- Patience: Maybe your Demas needs a little time to process and decide. If he rejects your initial overture, wait a month and then try again.

How do you deal with personal disappointment when Demas falls away?

- Take your disappointment to God. Read Psalms on a regular basis, for they are filled with encouragement and advice. Admit that you're angry and hurt.
- Refocus. Evaluate your goals and ministry expectations. Remember, many of your men may not possess your level of commitment yet.
- Refresh. Take some personal time with your family, do something fun, and spend some personal time with the Lord for encouragement.
- See the big picture. Stay committed to your vision and mission for ministry to men.

What happens when Demas undermines your leadership?

- Seek guidance. There is no better place to turn but to God's Word. Let me suggest you begin with Psalm 5.
- Take refuge. There is no better place when under attack than taking refuge in God (see Psalm 5:1–2).
- Pray personally and persistently (see Psalm 5:3).
- Stay up. In addition to personal prayer, pray with your leadership team and encourage one another. Keep them apprised of the situation so they know the truth.

How do you deal with ministry betrayal?

Sometimes Demas fights dirty. He intentionally attacks you and your ministry. Every great man of Scripture was at some point betrayed by someone he loved—and you will be too. Here is some advice:

- Avoid isolation. When Demas betrayed Paul, he summoned young Timothy: "Be diligent to come to me quickly"

(2 Timothy 4:9 NKJV). The apostle did not isolate himself; he chose to insulate his life with trustworthy friends.

- Move on. Jesus moved on with his mission and finishing all his Father sent him into the world to accomplish (see John 17:4).
- Trust God. Betrayal is a distraction that leads to destruction. Trust God to bring something good out of a bad situation. Read Genesis 50:20 and Romans 8:28–30.
- Document. You need to keep good records so that you can refute any false charges Demas may level at you and your ministry.

At what point do you give up on your Demas?

This is a difficult question to answer. Every situation is different. My advice is to keep praying for and approaching your Demas until he clearly says he no longer wants to have contact with you. As long as the door is ajar, keep knocking. If your Demas is actively undermining your ministry or spreading lies about you, you may need to cut ties and let the Lord deal with him (see 1 Corinthians 5:5).

Demas decided to walk away from ministry and ministerial associations. It was heartbreaking to not only the apostle Paul, but also to Dr. Luke. One can only hope that Demas came to his senses, rededicated his life to the Lord, and walked wholeheartedly with the Lord for the remainder of his time on earth.

As men's ministers, that's our goal for every man. The Lord is unwilling that any man should perish, but that all should come to repentance (2 Peter 3:9). God wants to redeem every man, even those who fall away. He wants to redeem even those who betray us.

42

FIT TO SERVE

(DAVID ASHLEY)

David Ashley, BSSM, MAA, MDiv (aka, "The Pastor of Pump"), has thirty years' experience as a fitness trainer (God's instrument to save bodies), which has led him into ministry as an evangelist, speaker, and discipler (God's instrument to help save souls). For more information, visit pastorofpump.com.

Paul wrote, "For while bodily training is of some value, godliness is of value in every way, as it holds promise for the present life and also for the life to come" (1 Timothy 4:8 ESV). We've all read this familiar verse. And I will be the first to say that spiritual disciplines are your priority. Spiritual training for godliness comes first.

But the inspired, inerrant, and infallible Word of God is clear—bodily training and physical well-being have value too. We teach, preach, counsel, and model the other aspects of Scripture, so why as ministry leaders do we pass over the value of physical exercise in our own lives?

Another familiar verse confirms, "Faith without works is dead" (James 2:26 NASB). In other words, faith requires action. Like a church without action, a body without action will eventually get sick and die. Action involves movement, and movement involves the heart, lungs, muscles, proper nutrition, and adequate rest. I am calling all fellow ministry leaders, as an act of worship, to transform the body given to you by God into a finely tuned machine.

Will adding a training program to your already-crazy schedule make a difference? A recent survey of ministry leaders by Francis A. Schaeffer Institute of Church Leadership Development revealed some not-so-surprising statistics:

- 54 percent are overworked and 43 percent are overstressed.
- 35 percent battle depression.
- 26 percent are overly fatigued.
- 18 percent work more than seventy hours a week and face unreasonable challenges.

If you don't have the strength and stamina to fulfill your responsibility as a pastoral leader or battle the demons of depression and anxiety, your ministry will suffer. If we are called to love God with all our heart, soul, mind, and strength, don't we want to give him our best? He gave us his best. Are we really okay with loving him with a heart that isn't 100 percent, a mind that can't remember things, or muscles that can't take up our cross? I think not.

We teach and preach about discipline and self-control, but isn't that hypocritical if we have a forty-four-inch waistline and body fat over 30 percent? How are we to be taken seriously on these subjects when we don't practice them ourselves? Could this be a sign of a bigger issue? Maybe ministry has become our idol and we have taken this to the extreme, losing balance in our life. The almighty Creator of heaven and earth has created us in his image and given us a body to steward for his glory.

As the great theologian Jimmy Buffet says, "I treat my body like a temple, you treat yours like a tent." If you are treating your temple like a tent, then I think you have a stewardship problem—and a stewardship problem leads to a worship problem.

You don't need a set of six-pack abs. I am talking about keeping your weight, waistline, and body fat in a safe and healthy range. As leaders, we should lead. Striving to be role models, not *roll* models. If you are not disciplined in your eating and exercise, you are telling your men that it is acceptable to live undisciplined lives. And we know that becoming lazy in one area of our lives often leads to becoming undisciplined and lazy in other areas.

Paul tells us to present our bodies as a "living sacrifice" (Romans 12:1). So what kind of sacrifice are you presenting? Is it optimal? Is it fit for a King? John Stott, in a sermon at Saddleback Church on October 30, 2005, said, "The authentic Christianity of the Bible is not safe, smug, cozy, selfish, or an escapist religion. On the contrary, it is deeply, disturbing to our sheltered security. It is an explosive ... force, which pulls us out from our narrow self-centeredness and flings us into God's world to witness to serve." The natural follow-up question for every man in ministry is this: *Are you fit to serve?*

The Bible tells us that when it comes to nutrition for our spiritual well-being, we need two things: bread and water.

> Jesus said to them, "I am the bread of life; whoever comes to me shall not hunger." (John 6:35 ESV)

> Jesus said, "But whoever drinks of the water that I will give him will never be thirsty again. The water that I will give him will become in him a spring of water welling up to eternal life." (John 4:14 ESV)

Eating and hydration are keys to being fit to serve. As I always tell my clients, "You can't out train a crappy diet." We must be conscious of what we are putting into our bodies. The modern-day adage is true: Garbage in, garbage out. Is that how you want to steward this gift from God? I hope not.

NUTRITION

Here are a few principles to follow when it comes to nutrition:

1. Eat four to six times a day, approximately every four hours. Snacks are preferable to larger meals.
2. Have a lean protein with each feeding. This increases metabolism and decreases hunger cravings.
3. Reduce your intake of sugar and processed foods. Fix your own meals and choose real food.
4. Eat a fruit and/or vegetable with each feeding.
5. Your complex carbs/starches should be primarily consumed for breakfast and after workouts.

Lean Protein	Vegetable	Fruit	Carbohydrate	Fat
Chicken Breast	Asparagus	Apple	Oatmeal	Almonds
Turkey Breast	Green Beans	Blueberries	Sweet Potato	Walnuts
Tuna	Broccoli	Pear	Whole Grain Bread	Extra Virgin Olive Oil
Flank Steak	Cucumber	Strawberries	Brown Rice	Butter
Protein Powder	Spinach	Plumb	Quinoa	Avocado
Egg Whites		Grapefruit		Coconut Oil

The benefits of a healthy eating plan are:

1. Increased energy and productivity
2. Decreased risk of heart disease, stroke, diabetes, and some types of cancer
3. Elevated mood
4. Regulated weight

HYDRATE

Drink more water! I can't stress this enough. Drink more water. Drink fewer—a lot fewer!—sugar drinks, diet sodas, juices, and caffeinated beverages. Drink more water. Are you tracking with me?

By properly hydrating your body, you will be less fatigued, more alert, perform better, think straighter, and just feel all-around great. Your goal should be to get between sixty-four to ninety-six ounces of water per day. The benefits of staying hydrated with water are:

1. Preventing fatigue
2. Helping reduce high blood pressure
3. Reducing digestive disorders
4. Helping maintain healthy weight
5. Slowing the aging process

EXERCISE

What if I told you moving your body thirty to forty minutes five times per week could help you lose weight, lower blood pressure, prevent depression, improve mood, improve sleep, and reduce stress and anxiety? Can I sign you up?

Cardiovascular Training

Choose your favorite. Then commit to running, jogging, walking, rowing, biking, swimming, elliptical, or any cardio workout two to three times per week. Set aside thirty to forty minutes per training session. Start easy, but work your way up to 70 percent of your maximum heart rate (220 minus your age = maximum heart rate). Then move eventually into interval type training.

Researchers at the University of British Columbia found that regular aerobic exercise seems to boost the size of the hippocampus, the area of the brain that is involved in verbal memory and learning. Sounds like something we all need as ministry leaders.

Strength Training

This includes free weights and body-weight training. Schedule two or three training sessions of forty minutes per week. Use complex, multijoint movements, along with core movements. Do five exercises for upper/lower body and two exercises for core. Use four sets of twelve to fifteen repetitions for the upper/lower, and twenty reps or timed sets for the core. Train hard enough to elicit a muscle burn and elevated heart rate.

In order to produce results with strength training and pumping iron, individuals must lift hard enough to irritate the muscle. That should come naturally to ministry leaders. When we mentor or disciple guys, we need to go deep with them and even cause a little irritation to produce growth. Here are some of the benefits of strength training:

1. It boosts your metabolism to burn more calories ... even at rest.
2. It boosts energy levels and improves your mood.
3. It is effective in disease prevention.
4. It protects bone health and improves posture.

REST AND RECOVERY

If you are doing ministry right, then you will be exhausted and worn out from the spiritual training and all the surprises that catch you during your ministry day. There's satisfaction knowing you went all in for King Jesus, and at the end of that day or week your body needs rest. Jesus rested after ministry, and so should we.

Take it from my experience—if you don't plan your rest, you *will* hit a wall. Burnout in ministry is becoming more prevalent, even among the younger generation of ministry leaders. So get a good seven to eight hours of sleep each night. There's also value in grabbing thirty- to sixty-minute naps. Also, schedule time to just get away and be alone with God. No cell phone, no television, no computer—just you, God, a Bible, and a notebook. Your physical and spiritual recovery are closely related.

Fellow ministers, none of this should come as a surprise to you. This book is filled with great ideas that require clear thinking, long hours of work, and significant energy. To get the most out of the ideas presented by the other contributors, you need to commit to a healthy lifestyle. I leave you with this: Your Bible says physical activity is of some value. It says to present your body as a living sacrifice. Gentlemen, will you worship God with excuses or with a healthy heart, a prayerful soul, a sound mind, and strength enough to carry your cross?

43

ALLOWING YOURSELF
TO BE DISCIPLED

(TOM GENSLER)

Tom Gensler is the director of ministry development for Relevant Practical Ministry for Men, a resource to the local church in the context of men's spiritual growth. Tom has been active in ministry to men for fifteen years, codirects four Iron Sharpens Iron conferences, serves as the adult ministry director in his local church, and leads Fathering Adventures, a transformational weekend camping experience. Learn more at rpmfm.org.

Doctors are notoriously bad patients; web designers often have terrible-looking homepages; the cobbler's children may have no shoes. You might call that vocational irony. Perhaps you, as a discipler of men, are failing to be discipled yourself. You spend so much time preparing talks, equipping small-group leaders, organizing outreach events, and meeting one-on-one with men who have real needs that you fail to nourish your own walk with Christ.

There are seasons in which you're on fire for Christ. The Holy Spirit leads with clarity, and you follow with joyful exuberance. Grace and purpose fill your life. You are touching the hearts and minds of men. It's a beautiful thing. But there are other times when you're running on empty. There's dissension among your troops. Cash is tight. Other ministries seem to get more attention. Doubts creep in. And things at home are not clicking. What do you do?

In good times and in bad times, you need to pursue a plan that feeds your deepest need: to know and receive God's love. To dig deep into his truth. To build relationship with your Creator and fellow believers. You need to allow yourself to be discipled. I'm speaking as a guy who has the privilege of rescuing other men only because I have been rescued myself. I can disciple only because I have been discipled.

I hope you agree that *disciple* is a verb. It was modeled by Jesus as he spoke into the lives of his closest followers. It's estimated that Jesus spent 85 percent of his time relationally connecting and *doing life* with his disciples. Yes, he spent time formally teaching, but he understood it was more important to connect head to head, heart to heart, modeling life on life.

I've been discipled by five solid, trustworthy men during the past ten years, men who understood how to connect relationally and who had a plan to help mature me spiritually. From their ongoing investments in me, I've been blessed to multiply this investment by becoming a discipler for more than twenty other men. That's no small commitment, but it is a direct response to Paul's challenge, "What you have heard from me in the presence of many witnesses entrust to faithful men, who will be able to teach others also" (2 Timothy 2:2 ESV).

To be clear, I did not meet with all five of these men and discuss the same things. For example, Tom Cheshire spent a year teaching me biblical manhood; Jeff Schulte spent a year really peeling back the layers of my heart to help me understand what was going on underneath the hood of my life. Bob Bolin meets with me nearly every week, and has for years, simply to pray with, love on, and encourage me to continue moving forward as a man of God.

DEVELOPING SOLID SPIRITUAL DISCIPLINES

In some sense, you have to earn the right—plow the field, so to speak—before you can even dare ask a busy, godly man to be your personal discipler. Why would a man commit to investing hours into your life if you haven't done the basics?

God finally got my attention regarding spiritual disciplines in 2007. My marriage bottomed out, and in that crucible, he confirmed three essential strategies I needed to embrace. It was not a coincidence that all five of my spiritual advisers practiced the same spiritual disciplines. As I grew into my own, drawing nearer to God and his Holy Spirit, I began my own daily focus on those three areas. I define them as P3 or The Power of Three.

Read the Bible with a Plan

It's surprising how many men's leaders are hit and miss with their quiet time. We all need to commit to a plan for grasping God's Word in its entirety. Do a 365-day reading plan, perhaps every year. Listen to an audio Bible. Use a proven plan from Back to the Bible or Logos Bible Software. Looking for a fresh start? As D. L. Moody said, "The Bible was not given for our information but for our transformation."

Pray with a Purpose

Saying, "Hey, brother, I'll pray for you," is one of the greatest gifts you can give, *if you follow through.* Too often, that's exactly what doesn't happen in today's fast-paced culture. Let's pledge to slow down … and write down our prayer promises and requests. Carry a prayer notebook and you'll be stunned how often your purposeful prayers are answered quite specifically.

Center Godly Men around You to Love and Gently Rebuke You When Needed

As recommended by Robert Lewis of Men's Fraternity, assemble your own personal board of directors. Humbly invite three or four men of integrity to hold you accountable, challenge you to seek God's best, and rebuke you as necessary. You may meet with some of these men regularly and some might be "on call." Their assignment is described in 2 Timothy 4:2: "Preach the word; be ready in season and out of season; reprove, rebuke, and exhort, with complete patience and teaching" (ESV).

Implementing the "Power of Three" is the foundation for your life and your ministry. Not coincidentally, out of your personal board of directors, you may very well find your own discipler.

IDENTIFYING A DISCIPLER

Identifying a discipler is no small task. A discipler-disciple relationship requires a robust commitment between two guys who get along, root for each other, and commit to meeting weekly for the long haul. Whom might you consider for this task? Make your own list of qualities you are hoping to add or enhance in your life—like courage, respect, honor, humility, curiosity, or confidence. One strategy is to make a list of adjectives. You may be seeking a discipler who is approachable, joy-filled, even-keeled, forgiving, and has a good sense of humor.

For me it was niceness. That may sound simplistic, but I spent more than a decade caught up in worldly ambition and had developed quite an aggressive killer attitude. God led me to a discipler who was just plain nice, and that was exactly what I needed. It also might be someone who has overcome some of the same challenges you are facing. You may be drawn to a man who overcame marriage challenges, substance abuse, a porn addiction, or a tragedy similar to something you have endured.

In most cases, the discipler is older than the disciple. Certainly, he has been actively following Christ longer. Initially, consider men in your church community, but you may find the right man on the job or in your neighborhood. Don't overlook that respected pastor or men's leader from across town. Maybe even another denomination! Also consider men you may not know well but who have a strong reputation. Friends of friends. Pastors of friends. Friends of pastors. Husbands of your wife's girlfriends.

Make a short list of guys you may want to ask. Then set it aside. Pray about it. See what God reveals through your own intuition and in the course of life. Without doing a complete background check, you may want to ask around to find out more about a few of your candidates.

Finally, when one name rises to the top, ask with confidence. Don't ambush him on the way into church. Instead, ask him to meet for coffee. You can already envision the conversation. First, acknowledge his stellar reputation. Talk a bit about your own walk with Christ. Share a couple victories and a few struggles. If he engages, then reveal that you're on a search for a mentor, spiritual advisor, or discipler. You'll know soon enough whether you should take the next step with this candidate or back off and just ask him if he has any recommendations.

If the conversation takes a turn toward pulling the trigger on an intentional discipling relationship, congratulations. Still, anticipate that the next month or two is really a trial period. If the match isn't right, no worries. Trust that God will teach you both something during that time and, after a break, resume your worthy quest.

THE DISCIPLING RELATIONSHIP

What does a discipler-disciple relationship look like? Let's begin by considering what it's not. It's not a friendship. It's not a teacher-student relationship. It's not an accountability partner. It's not just a two-person small group meeting or Bible study. There are elements of all the above. But mostly it's an intentional commitment to meet for the long haul with a man who will model integrity, ask you the tough questions, listen with discerning ears, and not let you settle for anything less than God's best.

I recommend you meet once a week, for about ninety minutes, at a place where you can freely talk. You may be surprised to hear that for the first six weeks or so, that's all you should expect to do. Just talk and get to know each other. Be real. Out of that time will come the transparency necessary for a legitimate discipling relationship

Soon enough, empower him—give him permission—to ask questions like, "What issues are you dealing with right now?"; "What's causing pain to you and the people you care about?"; and "What is God revealing in your life?" These are the kinds of empowering questions asked by those five men who wouldn't give up on me. These days, I ask those same type of questions of other men on a regular basis. In my ministry to men, I can help others clarify their vision only because I continue to identify my own weaknesses, flaws, gifts, and abilities.

In each session, address issues relating to your family, your ministry, your prayer and worship, and your spare time. Be willing to dig deep into any areas of struggle. When men meet one-on-one, it's easy to get distracted by sports scores, business frustrations, and talking about our kids. An hour or two can go by quickly. So get right to honest talk and relevant issues. Respect the process. If you go a few weeks *without* being corrected or rebuked, you're probably not being honest enough.

If it works, it's a win-win for both of you. And you could very well meet close to fifty times a year for a decade or more. I pray for that kind of relationship for you. That's not something to take for granted. Of course, even if you find the right person, there are all kinds of things that might knock your relationship off course. Job and schedule changes. Illness, personal challenges, and family conflicts. Be prepared to mourn that loss even as you celebrate your time together.

GENERATIONAL DISCIPLING

As you seek and submit to your own discipler, stay open to any younger man who comes to you and humbly asks you to meet with him as a spiritual advisor. That's a vital example of servant leadership. Generational discipling is the way ministry to men is supposed to work. Your family, church, ministry, outreach, and entire community will be stronger because of your commitment to humbling yourself, allowing your own cup to be filled, and then overflowing into the lives of others.

44

PRACTICAL STEPS TO A DAVID-JONATHAN FRIENDSHIP

(ROY ABBOTT)

Roy Abbott is the founder and president of Focal Point Ministries, a Christ-centered ministry focused on equipping and training leaders of men. For more information, go to focal pointministries.net.

When I was in junior high school, like most kids my age, I struggled with friendships. Whether real or imagined, I always seemed to be the odd man out. I worked hard to be accepted by the "cool" kids, often to my own peril. During one particularly difficult situation, my mother told me, "Roy, the way to have a friend is to be one."

At twelve years old, I had no real understanding of what she meant, but as I grew older, Mom's advice took root in my heart and soul and has become a foundational piece of my personal life and ministry. The foundational principle that has guided my life from that time on has been *everything boils down to relationships*.

In his book *Walden*, Henry David Thoreau notes, "The mass of men lead lives of quiet desperation." A man can be surrounded by people and yet desperately alone. Even though he has numerous friendships, the odds are high that no one really knows him. Too many men live without the experience of rich, meaningful relationships with another brother in Christ, and, to make matters worse, they often live in secrecy, bandaging any sin in their own lives because of that isolation.

As a leader of men, you know the importance of men building relationships with other godly men. You know spiritual growth and development happen only when men get real with one another. But as a leader, you also know that you can't teach what you don't know and you can't give away what you don't have. Perhaps that man in isolation is *you*. Perhaps you are living a Lone Ranger life with no close male friend to share a common bond with. If my hunch is right, it's not that you don't want friendships with other men; it's just that you're unsure of how to develop them.

In 1 Samuel 18 and 20, we read the story of Jonathan and David, two men who share a relationship that went deep—*very* deep. We see a friendship that transcended the superficial and dug into the core of these two men; a sacrificial relationship where one would lay down his life for the other.

FIVE FRIENDSHIP-BUILDING PRINCIPLES

In our heart of hearts, we all, as men, long for a friend who will stand by us through all the joys and sorrows of life; someone who will share in all of life's challenges and triumphs with us. How can any man develop those deep, healthy friendships our souls long for? The David-Jonathan relationship suggests five baseline principles.

Pray. First things first. This may be stating the obvious, but all too often prayer is overlooked *because* it is so obvious. Ask God to bring men into your life who will become your Jonathans; men who will have your back in any circumstance of life. Your ministry depends on it.

Be intentional. This may also seem obvious too, but the reality is that if you don't pursue a relationship with a level of intentionality, then it's never going to happen. You can't have something you're not willing to go after. Wishing it were true won't make it so.

I remember a time in my midthirties when I was working through some wounds surrounding my father. I was hurting because he didn't seem to "get it" when it came to a relationship with me. He was distant, and I desperately wanted him to reach out and talk to me and treat me as a son and as a friend. A wise man I counseled with and trusted looked me in the eye one day and said, "Your dad doesn't get it. If you want a relationship with him, *you're* going to have to go after him and get it yourself." I resolved right then and there to be intentional with him, to be the initiator.

To my surprise and delight, he slowly began to respond. I asked him questions and opened up my life to him, and he did the same. By the time he died ten years later, my dad and I had developed a wonderfully open relationship. I got to know my father because of my intentionality—and the grace of God.

Be transparent. Honesty is a key ingredient to building trust; in fact, you cannot build trust without being transparent. The more transparent we are, the more comfortable the other person will be to be able to share what's going on in his own life. Transparency is honesty, and honesty builds trust. Men tend to be suspicious and guarded when it comes to personal matters. You have to work to gain their trust. If your goal is to build friendships, expect to take the initiative and do much of the work. Again, I remember the wisdom of Mom: "If you want a friend, be prepared to do 90 percent of the work to get one."

Be patient. Building a trusting relationship takes time. It won't always be smooth sailing either. But stay with the process, and don't jump ship at the first sign of trouble. Oftentimes the deepest bonds are forged through working out issues or differences in the relationship.

Listen. We've all heard the adage "God gave us two ears and one mouth for a reason." Learn to listen and pay attention to what your friend is saying, rather than formulating your reply in your head as he is talking. Listening is a skill that is developed with practice.

Active listening honors the other person. Prior to vocational ministry, I spent many years in the nuclear power generation industry. On our plant property, we had two identical units generating electricity, and, because everything on unit two looked the same as on unit one, a maintenance worker or plant operator could easily get into the wrong unit to perform maintenance. The mistake could be catastrophic. Because of this, we had a three-way technique of communication by which instructions were repeated back to ensure they were heard correctly. This method required listening without thinking ahead of your own response. In relationship-building, you wouldn't want to be mechanical in your approach, but the repeating method still works. Use phrases like, "I heard you say …" and then repeat back in your own words what you heard)." A friend likes to know you listen, hear, and understand.

Look around. Your next friend could be anywhere. Look inside and outside your inner circle of men at your church. God may lead you to befriend a ministry leader or pastor across town or in the next county, perhaps even in another denomination. Consider the husbands of your wife's friends. When God opens a door, as stated earlier, be intentional—not desperate, but direct.

FREQUENTLY ASKED QUESTIONS

Here are a few other frequently asked questions for developing friendships.

The first is, *how often should we meet?* C. S. Lewis put it this way, "People who bore one another should meet seldom; people who interest one another, often."[1] In other words, this business of friend making should be joyous.

Establishing a close friendship is not the same as having an accountability partner. But still, you will want to be intentional about hanging out on a regular basis. If you don't meet often enough, you'll spend most of your time "catching up." I've met with a friend every Friday for lunch for several years now. He and I have a standing appointment. Sometimes a conflict arises, but normally we're committed to a sixty- to ninety-minute block of time together.

Where do we meet? Wherever there's food! Seriously, a restaurant is a good place to hang out. My friend and I started out our friendship by meeting together along the Mississippi River where we could have some solitude and privacy. This allowed us to get to that transparent place with one another and not compromise ourselves to others.

Does your time together always have to go deep? Of course not. Watching sports, playing sports, going to concerts, doing hobbies, or any shared interest can help lay a foundation for a lifelong friendship. Outings that includes wives can add another layer of mutual appreciation and understanding too.

What about the end of a friendship? That's going to happen. Seasons of life change. Priorities shift. The trust you've established should give you assurance that any private matters discussed stay confidential. If that's a concern, you may want to have a conversation establishing closure. But keeping lines of communication open may lead to a renewal of a rich relationship down the road.

FOR PASTORS ONLY

The following is an excerpt from an excellent article from ChristianityToday.com entitled "The Friendless Pastor" by Mark Brouwer:

> We mistakenly assume our relational needs can be met by people in our church. When I ask about friendships, most pastors I coach will talk about the people in their church that they get along with the best. For years that was my answer too. I worked to cultivate friendships with men in the church. I thought these friendships were healthy and helpful—and to a large extent they were. But I hadn't come to terms with the limitations of those relationships.
>
> People in the church are always looking to us to be their spiritual leaders and teachers, and this is a hat we can never take off. Because we have this responsibility, we will of necessity censor ourselves from sharing certain frustrations or concerns. Lingering in the back of our mind is the awareness that if we say something offensive or hurtful to this person, or express our frustrations about the church too candidly, it might impact their connection to our church, or it might come back to hurt our leadership.
>
> I know pastors who've been fired because of things they said to people they thought were friends during a time of personal openness and vulnerability. It's like the adage that is issued as a warning when you are interviewed by a journalist:

Be careful what you say, because whatever you say is "on the record." If you are a pastor, spending time with people in your church, whatever you say is on the record.

Consider the challenges of role confusion. We all recognize the dangers of trying to "be friends" with your children. Being a parent is different from being a buddy. The roles ought not be confused. Not only are our church relationships complicated because of the spiritual leadership dynamic, they are also complicated because of different, and sometimes conflicting, roles that we play in reporting relationships. Often pastors will identify people in their church as friends who are also church board members. These board members often have the task of deciding on compensation for, and sometimes the discipline and termination of, the pastor.

Can we have a completely transparent, reciprocal relationship with someone who looks to us as his spiritual teacher and leader or who serves in the role of corporate supervisor? It's highly unlikely.[2]

In his article, Mark Brouwer also warns that isolated leaders are more susceptible to temptation, discouragement, anxiety, sadness, and even bad decisions. The good news is that a leader can *diminish* those attributes by taking it upon himself to find and be a true friend. Don't settle for anything less.

45

A LESSON IN PERSEVERANCE

(JOE PELLEGRINO)

Joe Pellegrino is an author, speaker, life coach, and consultant. He is the founder of Legacy Minded Men (legacymindedmen .org), a group established to transform lives by engaging, encouraging, and equipping men to build a Christ-centered legacy. E-mail him at joe@legacymindedmen.org.

I love baseball. There isn't a better sight than a freshly cut ball field on a warm summer afternoon. No sound hits the eardrum like the pop of a glove or the crack of a bat.

I can trace my love for the game back to when I was ten years old. I'm the kind of guy who falls deeply in love with the things I appreciate. My passion for baseball is how I met Dave Swanson … more on that in a moment.

My other significant passion—in fact, my *first* significant passion—is for my Savior and Lord Jesus Christ. It took some time for me to understand my need for salvation and to grasp this passion, but once I did it became my ever-burning fuel. Once I became a Christian, in an effort to marry my two great passions—faith and baseball—I decided to write a book about Christian baseball players.

I assumed Christian players would be banging down my door to get into this book. But no such luck. Fortunately, one of my business associates was a former New York Yankee. He was able to wrangle me a copy of the Holy Grail: the Major League Baseball media guide. The guide contains highly private, inside information, like where players stay when travelling. And it was all mine. I was in my glory.

As I poured through this book, trying to absorb every ounce of knowledge I could, I saw a listing for something called Baseball Chapel. It was the perfect marriage of my two loves: faith and baseball.

Baseball Chapel is an organization that commissions chaplains to conduct short chapels for Major League teams and to work with players who seek discipleship. As I read on, I nearly collapsed. The headquarters for this fount of Christian-baseball goodness was located in Bloomingdale, New Jersey, fifteen minutes from my house! Fumbling for the telephone, I quickly dialed the indicated number, itching to talk to the organization's executive director, Mr. Dave Swanson.

Just as quickly as he had greeted me with, "Dave Swanson here," I spilled out my own introduction.

I said to him, "Mr. Swanson, I love the Lord and I love baseball. I was wondering if you could put me in touch with some Christian players." Silence on the other end.

"Why don't you go ahead and call me in three months," was his only reply.

Despite the eternity that three months would be, I acknowledged his request. When the calendar finally advanced to the date circled in red exclaiming "Call Dave Swanson," I dialed him again. To my surprise, he said again, "Call me in another three months."

Once again, I agreed and marked the date down on my calendar. After three more months had elapsed, I called him again. After a short time on the phone, I hung up. My wife asked what he had said. "Three more months," I replied. I was confused and annoyed—but nothing would stop me from getting the information I sought. If this was the man who had what I needed, I was sure as heck going to play by his rules.

A full year after my first phone call to Dave, I looked at the calendar. It was time to call and receive my three-month sentence yet again.

"Yes, Mr. Swanson. This is Joe Pellegrino, you asked me to call you back in three months regarding the names of Christian players."

His response: "Meet me at the Kin-Lon Diner in twenty minutes. "

I'm not sure if I even hung up the phone. Darting up the stairs and into my bedroom, I quickly changed from gym clothes into a pressed shirt and a tie. Within minutes of the invitation, I was on my way to the diner. When I arrived just on time, I found a tall, imposing, bald man of six foot three inches waiting for me at the entrance.

"Mr. Swanson?" I said. He nodded.

I stuck out my hand for a shake. Mr. Swanson held out a piece of paper. Then he turned toward the dining room to find a table. As I stared at him in amazement, I glanced down toward the sheet in my hand. On it were the names of Major League baseball players whom he considered strong Christian men. I couldn't believe it.

Before he could find a seat, I touched his shoulder. "Mr. Swanson," I said. "Forgive me, but why now? Why after a year?"

"Take a seat, Joe," he said, indicating a booth by the window.

As we sat, I was perked up and ready to listen intently. Mr. Swanson smiled. "My family owned the Thomas English Muffin Company. At one time, I was in charge of purchasing. Whenever a salesman called, I never bought from him the first time. If he came back a second time, I still did not buy from him. Nor did I do so if he came back a third time." Mr. Swanson's eyes were glued on mine. "But if the salesman persisted enough to return a fourth time, then he had a customer for life."

I learned a lesson in perseverance that day. It has served me well and has provided me with many sharing opportunities in the years that followed.

So often, we get struck down repeatedly. We feel rejected and helpless. Discouragement follows. In his letter to the Galatians, Paul writes, "Let us not become weary in doing good, for at the proper time we will reap a harvest *if we do not give up*" (Galatians 6:9). Giving up gets us nowhere. But if we persevere, keep our eyes on the goal, and keep running, we can experience that elusive place of convergence where success and purpose become one.

I did not realize it then, but the lesson Mr. Swanson taught me that day was one *I needed to learn*. This became obvious to me when I was led to start Legacy Minded Men (LMM), whose mission is to "transform lives by engaging, encouraging, and equipping men to build a Christ-centered legacy."

Moving men out of their comfort zone is difficult. As you know, men are fond of their habits, rituals, and routines. Month by month, I spoke with more and more men, sharing vision and receiving feedback. In the process, I realized we needed to line up volunteers if this organization was truly going to get off the ground. Just as before, I assumed Christian men would be banging down my door to be a part of LMM. No such luck. Building and managing a team of volunteers takes time, patience, and perseverance.

But even more difficult is the ongoing need to raise money to make the engine go. This is where perseverance is truly tested and pushed to its limits. At LMM, we often found ourselves short of cash. Several times we came down to the last day a payment needed to go out or a payroll was due. In the nick of time, we received an unexpected donation.

When you are in that situation, regardless of the amount of faith you possess, it grinds on you. There have been several times over the last six years when I thought about throwing in the towel. But every time I considered quitting, I would receive a phone call or e-mail or text message from a man who said how thankful he was for LMM.

That's why we do what we do. When God is driving the vision and lives are being changed, quitting is *not* an option. Unfortunately, too many quit when the fire gets too hot. They never realize the incredible blessing they could have received if only they had understood that the fire was refining and preparing them for the next battle.

Are you facing a difficult season in your ministry to men? I would urge you to embrace it—even if the flames are hot. You should love the assurance found in Hebrews 10:36: "For you have need of endurance, so that when you have done the will of God you may receive what is promised" (ESV).[1]

NOTES

Chapter 3

1   "Episode 28: John C. Maxwell," *Five Leadership Questions Podcast*, podcast audio, October 6, 2015, http://www.lifeway.com/leadership/2015/10/06/episode -28-john-maxwell/.

Chapter 8

1   Patrick Morley, David Delk, and Brett Clemmer, *No Man Left Behind* (Chicago: Moody Publishers, 2006).

Chapter 18

1   "The Effects of FatherFULLNESS," National Center for Fathering, http://www .fathers.com/statistics-and-research/the-effects-of-fatherfullness/.

2   "Parentless Statistics," Families Civil Liberties Union, http://www.fclu.org/parentless -statistics/.

3   "Unmarried Childbearing," National Center for Health Statistics, https://www. cdc.gov/nchs/fastats/unmarried-childbearing.htm.

Chapter 21

1   "Statistics on Pornography, Sexual Addiction, and Online Predators," Safe Families, http://www.safefamilies.org/sfStats.php.

2   Ibid.

3   "Pornography Statistics: Annual Report 2015," Covenant Eyes, http://www. covenanteyes.com/pornstats/.

4   Ibid.

5   "2014 Pornography Survey and Statistics," Proven Men Ministries, http://www. provenmen.org/2014pornsurvey.

Chapter 29

1   John Eldredge, *The Way of the Wild Heart* (Nashville, TN: Nelson Books, 2006), 280.

Chapter 31

1   Patrick Morley, *Pastoring Men* (Chicago, IL: Moody Publishers, 2009), 215.

2   John Ortberg, *The Me I Want to Be* (Grand Rapids, MI: Zondervan, 2009), 132.

3   Ibid., 134.

4   Richard J. Foster, *Prayer: Finding the Heart's True Home* (New York: Harper Collins, 1992), 15.

5   Ibid.

Chapter 34

1   "Unreached People Groups," Global Frontier Missions, accessed May 8, 2017, http://bit.ly/29Global.

2   Global Frontier Missions, "Missions Mobilization," accessed May 12, 2017, http://globalfrontiermissions.org/missions-mobilization/.

Chapter 38
1   Stephen Fishman, *Every Nonprofit's Tax Guide: How to Keep Your Tax-Exempt Status and Avoid IRS Problems* (Berkley, CA: NOLO, 2015).

Chapter 40
1   Excerpts from Josh McDowell, *10 Ways to Say I Love You* (Eugene, OR: Harvest House Publishers, 2015), chapter 2.

Chapter 44
1   C. S. Lewis, *The Four Loves* (New York: Harcourt Brace Jovanovich, 1960), 116.
2   Mark Brouwer, "The Friendless Pastor," ChristianityToday.com, http://www.christianitytoday.com/pastors/2014/march-online-only/friendless-pastor.html.

Chapter 45
1   Excerpts from Joe Battaglia and Joe Pellegrino, *That's My Dad!* (Racine, WI: BroadStreet Publishing, 2016).

ABOUT THE EDITORS

Jay Payleitner is one of the top freelance producers for Christian radio, producing *Josh McDowell Radio, Today's Father, Jesus Freaks Radio,* and *Project Angel Tree* with Chuck Colson. As a nationally known speaker, Jay has led marriage conferences and men's retreats, keynoted fundraising events, preached at weekend services, and spoken at Iron Sharpens Iron events in ten states. He is a longtime affiliate of the National Center for Fathering and served as Executive Director of the Illinois Fatherhood Initiative. Jay has sold more than half a million books, including the bestselling *52 Things Kids Need from a Dad* and *What If God Wrote Your Bucket List?* He has been a guest multiple times on *The Harvest Show, 100 Huntley Street,* and *Focus on the Family.* Track him down at jaypayleitner.com.

David Murrow is the best-selling author of *Why Men Hate Going to Church, What Your Husband Isn't Telling You, How Women Help Men Find God,* and *The Map: The Way of All Great Men.* He is also the founder of Church for Men, an organization that helps congregations reach more men and boys. His website is ChurchForMen.com.